IRRESISTIBLE LEARNING

EMBEDDING A CULTURE OF RESEARCH IN SCHOOLS

GRAHAM CHISNELL

First Published 2021

by John Catt Educational Ltd,
15 Riduna Park, Station Road,
Melton, Woodbridge IP12 1QT

Tel: +44 (0) 1394 389850
Email: enquiries@johncatt.com
Website: www.johncatt.com

ISBN: 978 1 913622 62 6

Set and designed by John Catt Educational Limited

To Lucy, James, Tom and Rebecca, who continue to teach me more than I could ever imagine possible.

Contents

Acknowledgements   7
Foreword   9

Chapter 1: Introduction   11
Chapter 2: Research Methodology   17
    Step 1: Define the issue   19
    Step 2: Build a question to answer the issue   25
    Step 3: Review what is known about the issue   31
    Step 4: Refine the question   53
    Step 5: Select the research methodology   56
    Step 6: Analyse the findings   84
    Step 7: Share the new understanding   97
    Step 8: Adapt or affirm practice in light of what you have learnt   104
Chapter 3: Creating a culture of research   111

Conclusion   151
Bibliography   153

Acknowledgements

Lucy, for tolerating the late evenings. To James, Tom and Rebecca for teaching me new things every day.

Frazer and John for your encouragement and critical eye on my many iterations of this book. Kerry for being the Ant to my Dec at our TeachMeets.

My work family – Mel, Jan, Nikki, Jon, Martin, Annie, Anne-Marie, Rob, Adam, Alison and so many remarkable people who have been there to tolerate my terrible jokes and share my laughs and tears.

My teachers, including Mr Key, Mr Holmes and Miss Birkett of Old Hall Junior school, who fuelled my love for music, maths and laughter. Amrik Marwaha and Dave Grafton of Chesterfield Boys' School, who built my interest in science. Georges Dussart and Keith Sharpe of Canterbury Christ Church College, who helped me discover myself as a teacher and researcher. To you and all my teachers who have inspired me on this winding pathway.

Foreword

Graham Chisnell compellingly describes the way in which he has built a culture of enquiry and research across his schools. He modestly presents a detailed Research Cycle that describes the process of engaging with research and refining questions that ultimately lead to new shared understanding. Building culture is a continuous process and relies on the leadership team fostering the key disposition of openness. Where the leadership team value ideas, are open to possibilities and are willing to be surprised, they are predisposed to enabling enquiry and research to inform decision-making. Throughout this text, we see the hugely positive outcomes of this leadership style.

When I worked as a headteacher, I was privileged to also work alongside a team of external researchers from the University of Cambridge. We recruited teachers, teaching assistants, children and parents from within our school community to study our vision for teaching without labelling by 'ability'. As headteacher, I took on the role of insider-researcher, conducting interviews, keeping a leadership journal and meeting regularly over a period of years with the research team as we prepared to write a book about the alternative school improvement journey that was taking place (Swann et al., 2012). We began this process soon after my appointment, when the school had only recently been removed from 'special measures'. The external research team worked with the school for a period of three years before moving to the analysis and dissemination phase. Looking back, I now realise that the process of transformation and school improvement that took place was a direct result of the power of a collective mission to question and move away from a limiting assumption that there is a 'right way' of doing things. A school that focuses on the kinds of deep questions that Graham outlines is one where easy answers are almost never going to help.

The listening school ethos that we created was deeply influenced by core principles of trust, co-agency and inclusion. The school community embraced an open approach where every member of the team (both children and adults) knew that their ideas and opinions mattered and would be taken into account. So many of the dispositions for learning that we uncovered in our research echo powerfully within this book.

As you read on, do so with openness. Remember the importance of restlessly questioning, deploying creativity in response to challenge, persisting with courage and humility. Recognise that a climate of emotional stability enables risk-taking and that generosity fosters the capacity to welcome difference in a spirit of mutual supportiveness. The culture you create as a leader within your classroom, your department or across your school will be so much richer if you have the courage to explore beyond 'what' is happening towards 'why'.

Dame Alison Peacock
Chief Executive of the Chartered College of Teaching

Swann, M., Peacock, A., Hart, S. and Drummond, M. J. (2012) Creating Learning without Limits. Maidenhead: Open University Press.

Chapter 1
Introduction

'Education is not the learning of facts, but the training of the mind to think.'
Albert Einstein

I unwrapped my first guitar, a classical acoustic, on my 11th birthday. The science lab technician at my school ran a guitar club at lunchtime and helped me grapple with the basics. I then enrolled with a guitar tutor, Steve Marsh, who was an inspiring classical acoustic guitarist. He taught me how to read guitar music and to challenge myself. I wasn't the best student as I didn't practise enough. I found the discipline of reading music cumbersome. I was now 14 years old, and as I apologetically unzipped my guitar case and fumbled my way through the piece I should have been practising, Steve stopped me. 'Graham,' he said, 'I'm not sure your heart is in this.' I agreed and told Steve that I had spent the week composing a song. Steve asked me to play the song to him. He then suggested that I should focus on developing my guitar skills through composition, and from this point, my musicianship took an upward turn. I used the key skills I had learnt through classical training and started to use arpeggios and the finger work on the fretboard Steve had taught me to add texture and tone to how I played. I played along to familiar songs; I composed; I sang; I lost myself in what Ken Robinson (2009) would call my 'element'. I became lost in the moment when I played and time seemed to curve, and in this space, thoughts appeared and songs formed.

I then moved away from my hometown of Chesterfield in Derbyshire and began my first year at teacher training college in Canterbury. My passion for music continued. While I studied for a joint honours degree in education and science, the college had a music department and therein a smattering of musicians keen to start a band. We created a folk band called Reason for the Echo. The band used original material composed by band members and we had the best of times.

I got to the end of my first year at college and sat my first exams. While my submissions during the course of the year were reasonably successful, my exams were not. I was about to experience my first key moment of revelation that would inform my journey in educational research. I was called in to see the dean of education, Margaret Alfrey. Margaret was an old-school dean who believed deeply in the nurturement of future teachers. She sat me down in her office and looked at my exam submission. 'Well, Graham,' she said with a gentle exhale as she fixed my eye. 'It appears one of two things are happening here. With your coursework submission, you are on track for an upper second, while your exam is as close to a fail as you could muster. Either your submissions indicate you have taken a plagiaristic route or you simply haven't learnt how to sit written exams.' I gave her my best nervous smile and said, 'I'll take the latter option.'

'Well,' she said with a wry smile, ushering a book across the table to me, 'you had best read this before taking your next exam.' The book (whose author, I am sad to say, I do not recall) told me some simple steps in how to revise, assuring me that I didn't need to recall every detail, but rather a range of key information as I entered the exam room. This was a revelation to me, and I used the skills in the book to prepare, with friends, for the next exam. How did it go, I hear you ask? Well, I have never been an A* student and have always had to graft to get half-decent results, so with concerted effort and an acquired set of study skills, I graduated with an upper second joint honours degree in 1994.

It often takes three key moments of revelation before learning truly sticks. For my second, let me take us forward six years from my conversation with the dean of education. I was in my first appointment as a primary school teacher at Reculver Church of England Primary School in Herne Bay. I had been appointed as music coordinator and had met with the deputy headteacher to request sponsorship in enrolling for the part-time master's degree course in expressive arts. The course matched my role as music coordinator and the taught parts of the course were held at weekends or during school holidays so wouldn't impact on my teaching. Having been a scientist who dropped all arts lessons at the age of 14, Carol, my deputy headteacher, thought this a curious step. Nonetheless, she met with Simon, my headteacher, and returned with the joyful news that the school would sponsor my course fees. I felt overjoyed to work in a school that valued the training and development of a fledgling member of staff. I enrolled on the course and had to work exceptionally hard to understand a discipline which I had little prior knowledge of. I read fervently: articles, books and journals. This was the mid-1990s, before internet searches were readily available, so my time was spent in the archives of the college library thumbing through journals and books. I visited art galleries and theatres to see the theoretical words I had read come to life. I was building a body of knowledge and understanding about arts in education that complemented my understanding of science.

Now to the third key moment of revelation. Although I had studied at master's level in a new discipline, my practice in school had not significantly changed. I continued to follow the national curriculum and national schemes of work produced by the Qualification and Curriculum Authority (QCA). I had honed my knowledge of the arts through reading books and journals, building an understanding of the research of others. I had devised clever research questions to interrogate and deepen my understanding of the complexities of the arts in education. I had analysed the findings of my research. However, the final and most pivotal step was absent. I had not shared my findings with others within my school and consequently, my practice and the practice of others had not changed as a result of my newly found knowledge. Herein lies the power of research in schools and the pathway to transformational change. The revelation sunk in: in order to create a culture of research in our schools, we must build the skills in staff to research well, to pose purposeful research questions, to seek what is already known, to carefully plan how we test out a relevant research question and to share the findings in order to inform future practice.

For me, building a culture of research follows a similar pathway to my journey with the guitar. While I had to go through the laborious task of developing my research skills, once mastered, research practice in school becomes a joy and an inspiration. I now take my staff along a research pathway that provides them with techniques that build research habits to help develop research skills. The application of these research skills helps create a culture of research that pervades the whole organisation.

Whatever your role in school, whether you are leading research practice or developing this in your own practice, this book is for you. The hope is that through deepening your awareness of the practice I share, you can align your existing practice to build a culture and climate of research that pervades all you do within your classroom, department, school, trust or organisation. It is also worth noting at this point that when I refer to 'researchers', I do not limit this noun to teachers. In my organisation, and I would suggest in yours, every employee is a researcher and engages in research, whether they operate in the curriculum or business teams.

I will provide a pathway to help embed a culture of research in your school. By following the steps within this book, you will build a vibrant organisation of highly motivated staff who are research active. Moreover, you will create a culture of self-improvement that is tailored to your contextual needs, bringing relevance and purpose to your strategic development.

I will take you through two phases in building a culture and climate of research. Firstly, I will guide you through the eight steps of the Research Cycle as a tool to structure your research practice, building your capacity for research and deepening a culture of research across your practice and that of your organisation. Secondly, I will help you to build systems that embed a culture of research that empowers staff at every level within your organisation.

What is research?

> **research:** *a detailed study of a subject, especially in order to discover (new) information or reach a (new) understanding*   Cambridge Dictionary

Research means many things to different people. To an academic writing up their doctoral thesis, research can be complex and involve strict protocols. To the staff member in a busy school, research may be more fluid and involve answering a key question to help improve their practice. Research involves finding out about an element of practice; this helps the researcher to become increasingly aware of the practice and opens their mind to multiple points of view. In knowing more about an element of practice, the researcher can then start to form meaningful questions of interest to their role within the school. But forging a great research question is not as easy as it sounds: the researcher will need to draw on their knowledge of what is already known about their field of study in the research of others. Once the question has been refined into a great research question, the researcher is now ready to engage in the research that will lead them to new understanding. This new understanding empowers the researcher to challenge their own practice or the practice of others. The researcher is then led to one of two options: to affirm their practice or change their practice. This is the essence of research-informed practice.

While we mustn't get bogged down by an elitist view of research, there are important steps to the research process that ensure there is validity in your research findings. I have devised a practical structure for research in schools called the Research Cycle that will take you through eight key steps that will strengthen your research and impact on your future practice. The Research Cycle will help you build a culture in which research across the school community can be realised by you and all staff. To be clear, by 'all staff' I do mean all staff employed by the organisation, not just teachers or those staff working in classrooms. In my schools, every member of staff is a researcher.

Why engage in research?

Building a culture of research in school empowers staff at every level to influence and play an active role in the strategic development of the organisation. The effect of this is fourfold. Relationships are strengthened by the conversations about research practice and outcomes. The culture of the school is enhanced as a result of transformational change introduced from the research findings. The quality of provision is improved through the necessity to engage with research findings, leading staff to use their findings to continue good practice and adapt it in light of what they have learnt and to drop practice that is no longer effective. And the heart of the school beats stronger as staff and pupils sense the pride in belonging to an organisation that shows an enquiring interest in what it does. In my trust, we encapsulate these four elements in the phrase 'irresistible learning for all'. This builds an organisational commitment to research for all staff through a shared belief that research practice improves outcomes for students.

Key messages from chapter 1 – 'Introduction'

- **Research is a detailed study of a subject**, especially in order to discover **new information** or reach a **new understanding**.
- Research means **many things** to different people.
- Research in school **empowers** the researcher to **challenge their own practice**, adapting practice as a result of what is learnt.
- **Every member of staff** in school can be a researcher.
- Building a culture of research in school empowers staff at every level to influence and play an **active role** in the strategic development of the organisation.
- Research builds four key elements in a school – **relationships are strengthened**, the **environment is enhanced**, the quality of **provision is improved** for students and the **heart of the school beats stronger** than ever before.

Chapter 2
Research Methodology

Our technical skills as researchers need to be nurtured if we are to ensure research in school is purposeful and has the potential to bring about a transformational change. As we hone our research skills, our proficiency as researchers grows; so too does our enjoyment and passion for research. Returning to my story in the introduction, by learning the technical skills of playing the guitar, I was able to deepen my joy of musicianship. This mirrors the importance of developing a technical understanding of research methodologies. Our passion for and enjoyment of research deepens with the technical understanding of the tools of research. In this chapter, I will explore eight key steps of research methodology and provide a structure to research that is accessible by all staff within school. These eight steps will help you to build a solid foundation of research practice that will strengthen your research outcomes and enhance your passion for research-informed practice.

In order to develop confidence as a researcher in school, we must start by demystifying what is meant by 'research'. Research can appear intimidating and untenable to many staff within schools. Research is often seen as only in the purview of graduates or restricted to those who are actively enrolled at university. This must be challenged, as research is not an elitist construct; it is a practice that is accessible to you and all who work in schools. I tell my staff that research involves asking and interrogating an interesting question and sharing what you find out with others. By presenting research as a process of being professionally curious, we start to see it as attainable, manageable, relevant and interesting. Moreover, we start to view ourselves as researchers.

Another important factor in introducing a culture of research in schools is to provide a research coach. The research coach works with the staff member to encourage, clarify the process of research and build confidence as a researcher. The research coach delivers sessions on research methodology and then follows this up through discussions and engagement. This creates the culture of an evolving conversation around the research undertaken and strengthens the heart of the school to beat stronger with every conversation. In order to bring research to the practice of all staff in school, I have devised the Research Cycle as a reference tool to support staff on their pathway of research.

The Research Cycle

The Research Cycle consists of eight steps that the researcher follows in order to structure their research. The cycle, while flexible, often takes one academic year to complete. This allows research to align to your appraisal cycle while ensuring the research activity is not rushed. Each step supports and strengthens your research skills and practice. The full cycle is shown in the pictogram below.

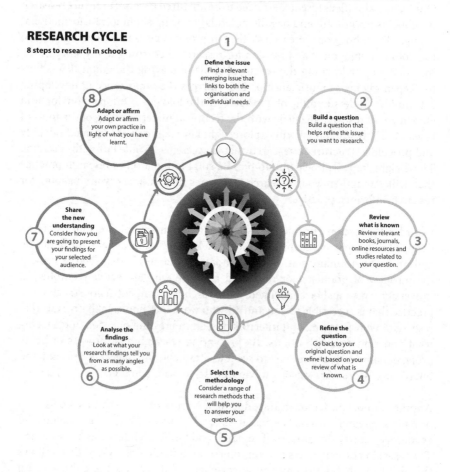

RESEARCH CYCLE
8 steps to research in schools

1 Define the issue
Find a relevant emerging issue that links to both the organisation and individual needs.

2 Build a question
Build a question that helps refine the issue you want to research.

3 Review what is known
Review relevant books, journals, online resources and studies related to your question.

4 Refine the question
Go back to your original question and refine it based on your review of what is known.

5 Select the methodology
Consider a range of research methods that will help you to answer your question.

6 Analyse the findings
Look at what your research findings tell you from as many angles as possible.

7 Share the new understanding
Consider how you are going to present your findings for your selected audience.

8 Adapt or affirm
Adapt or affirm your own practice in light of what you have learnt.

THE RESEARCH CYCLE
Step 1: Define the issue

In the cacophony of our daily lives in school, there is often a great deal of distracting noise. Not simply from the students we teach but from the myriad of unresolved tasks that fill our minds. Cognitive load theory (Sweller, 1998) is rooted in the concept that our working memory – the part of our mind that processes what we are currently doing – can only deal with a limited amount of information at any given time. Cognitive load theory helps us to articulate the diminishing ability to think when our minds are filled to the brim with noise (Lovell, 2020). In order to take the first step on the research journey, we must try our hardest to reduce this noise. We need to help ourselves as researchers to focus on the issues we face and to move beyond what Daniel Kahneman would call 'lazy' or 'fast thinking' (Kahneman, 2011). It would be easy to think of an issue we face and accept our first and most present thought, especially if our working memory is filled to capacity. However, while this most pressing issue may be relevant to the moment, it may not be at the heart of the systemic issue that affects our practice.

As an example, let us imagine our researcher to be a teaching assistant who is struggling with the ability to help an autistic student manage their behaviour in class. To the teaching assistant, this is an immediate issue to resolve and an issue that is causing both them and their student anxiety. There is a real urge for the teaching assistant to rush to find a solution to the misbehaviour of the student without carefully thinking about the wider factors impacting on the student's behaviour. But by carefully defining the issue, the researcher is led to a wider perspective of the issue they face. In this example, the teaching assistant is guided to think about the wider factors affecting the student's behaviour, such as their home environment, class environment, relationships with their peers, relationships with the adults in the room, the smell of the classroom, residual noise levels, or a myriad of other unseen factors. In order to help the teaching assistant go beyond the first and most immediate or obvious issue, we must encourage them to dig more deeply into their thinking, to unpack any bias in their understanding of the issue and to move to what Daniel Kahneman would call 'slow thinking'. Slow thinking is the deliberate act of recognising that the initial or most immediate response to a thought or question may contain either conscious or unconscious bias, leading to a swift and often over-simplified response. Encouraging our teaching assistant in this example to start slow thinking is the important step into moving them from being reactive to becoming research-informed.

In order to define the issue worthy of research, both the time and place for thinking need to be considered. The distracting noise that every employee in a school faces needs to be muted, enabling the cognitive load to reduce and providing space in your working memory to think. The starting point to help mute this organisational noise is to find a quiet spot, away from your usual routine, to have a coaching conversation. In creating the uninterrupted place to have a conversation that goes beyond fast thinking, you are afforded the space to find a meaningful issue that could evolve into an engaging research question. This place should be beyond distraction, be a treasured time for you and your research coach, and be a regular entitlement for you and all staff in school.

While there are many ways in which you can create the space for 'slow thinking', I use the appraisal system to formalise a time to meet. I put aside one hour; this is an embedded element of the appraisal cycle for our organisation. The coaching conversation uses dialogic questioning (Alexander, 2020) and engages the researcher in a focused discussion about their previous year's research, unpacking what went well, the bumps in the road they experienced and how their research outcomes impacted upon their own practice or the practice of others. We then move on to a dialogue about the current challenges the researcher faces and explore the context of these challenges.

A potential research issue can arise at any point in the year and may not present itself at the start of the appraisal cycle. You also need the flexibility to seize the moment when presented with an opportunity to define a potential research issue. Let us go back to the example above, where the teaching assistant faces an immediate issue regarding the behaviour of their autistic student. This issue may arise mid-year and not align to a more formalised cycle of appraisal or research. In such cases, both researcher and research coach need to be agile. In this example, the coach can meet with the teaching assistant to help them define the issue. Again, finding the right time and place for this discussion is important in order to allow thinking space for the teaching assistant. The coach could ask the teaching assistant to explain their issue and then offer questions that will help them unpack the context of their issue. This form of coaching in the moment can be very powerful for the researcher and help them find clarity in building a helpful research question to explore. Research opportunities can therefore be both incidental or planned within a more formal cycle of research in schools.

I have been a mentor-coach trainer for a number of years and use these skills to train our appraisal leaders in key techniques to facilitate 'slow thinking'. A technique we apply to the first step of the research process is Cooperrider and Srivastva's (1987) 'appreciative inquiry' model. Appreciative inquiry asks the researcher to think through their current perceived strengths. The researcher is asked to focus on their successes and positive outcomes within their practice. Any talk of negative issues or self-deprecation is quickly halted; only positive comments are permitted at this stage in the dialogue. Questions at this point are inquisitive and lead the researcher to think about their current strengths in practice. Let's pick up the narrative of our teaching assistant who is considering the issue of behaviour of their student. The coach may ask questions such as:

- What has **worked well** for you this year in developing outcomes for the students you support?
- What do you **enjoy most** about your role as a teaching assistant?
- Talk to me about your **most effective strategies** to engage autistic students.
- What would your students say your **greatest strengths** are as a teaching assistant?
- What strategies for behaviour seem to **work best** with students with autism?

At this point, it is worth drawing further on the skills of a research coach. I had the privilege of working with Roger Pask, who coached me in mentor-coaching skills. In this process, Roger spoke about the necessity to 'attend to the mentee' (Joy and Pask, 2007). The process of 'attending to the researcher' encourages the research coach to lose themselves in the moment and be present with the researcher. With this in mind, the research coach must hold their assumptions lightly, recognise what cognitive bias they bring to the conversation, and be prepared to ask searching Socratic questions, without the compulsion to answer these on behalf of the researcher but rather providing the space in which the researcher can contemplate their own response.

The appreciative inquiry dialogue now moves on to ask questions about the researcher's current unresolved issues. Once again, the researcher needs to be encouraged, through skilful dialogic questioning, to move to slow thinking. The research coach must ensure they do not allow the researcher to be satisfied with their first thought or response. They need to question beyond the immediate and obvious issues and test out assumptions that are made by the researcher, helping the researcher to shine a light on their own conscious or unconscious bias. With our teaching assistant, the coach could ask the following questions:

- **Tell me about** the current behaviours of your student.
- Which of these behaviours are **affecting you?**
- **Why do you think** this is affecting you?
- **What factors do you think** may be influencing your student's behaviour in school, at home, with peers?
- What triggers these behaviours? **Is there a pattern here?**
- Is there any other issue that may be **getting in the way** of making your influence on your student effective?

These questions may be helpful to elicit slow thinking and help the researcher move beyond their first and most immediate thought. The questions also start to unpack the researcher's unconscious biases or assumptions about what they think may be happening with the behaviours of the student or indeed their own practice. So, if you are on your first steps of research, find a research coach or use these questions to prompt your own thinking as you approach a potential issue for research.

It is worth noting that this initial conversation about the issues you are facing may not lead to a clarity of understanding that prepares you for step 2 in the Research Cycle, building a question to answer the issue. If this happens, don't worry. Thinking slow can take time, and at this stage, if there is further clarity needed, you can return to the conversation with your research coach after you have had time to reflect on your thinking, talk to colleagues or read relevant texts that could help. It is better to gain a clarity of understanding of the issues you face than to rush the process.

Once the issue is defined, you need to question the validity of your issue as a potential research area. Does the issue resonate with your interest and practice? Does the issue, and a deepening understanding of this issue, have the potential to resonate with other staff within the school, department, trust or network of schools? Does the issue help the school's own direction of travel and have the potential to benefit the organisation as a whole? The research coach, speaking with the teaching assistant, could say, 'I can see that the issue you have defined regarding your student is one that many other staff will find interesting across the trust. This could really help develop our understanding of how best to support our students with autism,' thus emphasising genuine purpose in the issue for both the researcher and the organisation.

It is vital that you take ownership of the issue and subsequent research and consider it relevant and important. A heavy-handed approach by a research coach may direct you to an area of research which you feel is not relevant to your practice. In such cases, you need to articulate this clearly to your research coach. A skilled research coach or appraisal lead should allow their researcher to guide their definition of the issue. Overbearing influence from the research coach at this stage can lead to you feeling that you have been strong-armed into a research project that, while relevant for the organisation, has limited relevance to your role. This is where an organisation-wide understanding of the Research Cycle is pivotal in building the right culture for research.

It is important that the issue and subsequent research is within the roles and responsibilities of the researcher and is relevant to the organisation. There is a danger that, should the issue oppose the organisational values or strategic direction, the researcher will swiftly discover they are not allowed to undertake the research because the issue is beyond their roles and responsibilities or because it may take them away from their organisation's core focus. As an example, a teaching assistant may have a personal interest in discussing an issue relating to the impact of the classroom environment for pupils who have Tourette's syndrome but not have any pupils with Tourette's syndrome at their school. Or indeed the teaching assistant may be attempting to direct their time to work away from what they have been tasked to do in support of pupils within their own class. For these reasons, the research coach must be mindful of any bias, be it conscious or unconscious bias, from the researcher. The research coach must ask their researcher how the issue relates to their roles and responsibilities and to the organisational priorities as this helps to ensure there is both meaning and purpose to the research project. Equally, as a researcher, you must remain honest and alert to your own bias when defining an issue for research and try to seek an issue that is relevant to both your own interests and those of the organisation.

At this point in your thinking, you will have discussed a myriad of potential issues and funnelled these down to one or two. You need to then ask yourself these three key questions to test out whether the issue is a worthy research area:

- Is the issue I have defined relevant to me?
- Is the issue I have defined relevant to my organisation?
- Will researching this issue help to develop my practice?

If the answer is yes to these questions, it is time to move on to defining a research question that will help unpack this issue. It is time to move to step 2 of the Research Cycle.

Key messages from step 1 'Define the issue'

The cycle of research in schools starts with **defining an issue that is relevant** to you and the organisation and that will potentially help to improve your practice or the practice of others.

- **Find time** to meet with a research coach to still the distracting noise, enabling you to think about the professional issues you face.
- Use **appreciative inquiry** to help you recognise strengths in your practice that can inform your research question.
- **Think slow** in order to go beyond your initial thoughts and ideas.
- Address your own **assumptions and biases** related to your research issue.
- Meet with a research coach who will ask **questions to encourage you to think**, while allowing you to own your issue without being strong-armed into research that may lack relevance to you.
- **Funnel down** the issues you face and focus on one relevant and accessible issue that is purposeful to your professional roles and responsibilities.

THE RESEARCH CYCLE
Step 2: Build a question to answer the issue

Once you have spent time grappling with the context of research in step 1 of the Research Cycle, it is now time to build a question to answer the issue. This process can often be hampered by fast thinking (Kahneman, 2011). Jumping at the first question that springs to mind may lead to difficulties in later research as the question could be too broad, overly vague, biased or just plain boring. The question needs to have purpose, and you need to ensure the question leads you towards the desired outcome of your research: an improvement in or affirmation of your practice. Keep the end point in view, or at least a presumption of what the end point may look like. If you settle on the wrong question, there is a real danger that the research will lead you to an end point that lacks purpose or relevance to your practice.

Gary Thomas (2017) suggests there are four types of research questions and defines these as:

1. What's the situation?
2. What's going on here?
3. What happens when?
4. What is related to what?

These help you to define a purposeful question.

What's the situation?
The first of Thomas's questions asks you to simply describe what you are observing. This is a helpful starting point for the researcher's first steps into research in schools. Returning to our teaching assistant who has an issue regarding the behaviour of an autistic student, consider the question 'What are the different strategies for supporting the behaviour of a student with autism?' At first sight, this is a helpful question to allow the teaching assistant (who may be new to post) explore the different strategies for supporting a pupil with autism

within the class. The question may, however, require further clarification. The question does not yet help the researcher to define the situation they face. As such, the researcher may need to refine their question to ensure it aligns to the desired outcome of their research.

Taking this example, the researcher needs to be more specific about their first research question. The research coach could ask:

- Is there a particular subject area that would be of interest to your research question?
- Is there a particular time of day when negative behaviours escalate?
- Are there any other factors that change at the same time as the behaviour escalates?
- Is there any difference in the routines in lessons when the behaviour escalates?
- Are there any particular physical clues that indicate heightened anxiety in the student?

Here, the research coach is trying, through these questions, to help the researcher to narrow their field of study in order to make their research more manageable and the outcome more impactful. With a narrower focus on this descriptive question, the researcher has a greater chance to find out something of interest that will impact positively on their practice and potentially the practice of others. Through further coaching and questioning, the researcher is then led to a more refined research question: 'What are the factors that influence an escalation in negative behaviours of an autistic student?' This question allows our researcher to step back, take a wider view and ask what the situation is.

Thomas draws an analogy between this style of question and painting a picture. He states that the researcher should, through their research question and subsequent research, be able to paint a picture of what is happening through words. As with any painting, however, it is provided through the lens of the artist, and this is also the case in research. As a researcher, you can put your own interpretation on the research, making it unique to your setting and own interests. This is not something to shy away from, but something to embrace. Provided you name your own perspective in this research and highlight your own potential bias, this style of research question can be effective.

What's going on here?

The 'What's going on here?' style of question asks the researcher to question beyond their observation of the issue. Thomas likens this to shining a spotlight on a darkened area of understanding. The spotlight, being metaphorically the research question, allows the researcher to illuminate a key part of their practice that is currently not fully understood. Thomas puts this well as he writes:

> First, it means that you are expecting to see something that you couldn't see before. Second, it implies also that you will be able to see because you are looking in a way that you weren't able to previously. Third, it implies you are giving time and energy to looking hard (i.e. shining the light) and using *your own self* – your intelligence and experience – to make sense of the subject under study. (Thomas, 2017)

Returning to our teaching assistant who is grappling with the behaviour of an autistic student in their class, they ask about an element of their practice, forming the question, 'Why does an autistic student in my intervention group struggle to stay on task in maths lessons?' The question now asks the researcher to discover what is not known about the situation rather than simply describing what is seen. It challenges the researcher to consider the factors that effect a change in the behaviour of the student. As Thomas states in the quote above, the researcher is led to bring their own reasoning and experience to their observations of the student in order to make sense of what is going on.

What happens when?

The 'What happens when?' question, Thomas suggests, involves the researcher considering two or more observations. This could be what happens before and after implementing a change in practice. An example of this for our teaching assistant may be asking the question, 'What happens to the behaviour of my student in maths lessons when I introduce a mindfulness session before the lesson?' This research question allows the researcher to try to define the impact of one or more factors on a pupil's development. Thomas puts this simply in the phrase, 'Does X cause Y?'

Widening the use of this style of questioning, at a strategic level in school, a member of the senior leadership team could pose a question that asks whether the introduction of a no-marking policy helps reduce teacher workload. While this is a simple question, the researcher needs to be aware of its limitations. The researcher's bias may get in the way as the senior leader may not have an accurate understanding of what teachers currently feel about their workload and whether marking is a significant factor in their perception of workload. The researcher may get different answers to this question from different year group colleagues. The question may be answered differently by the same member of staff depending on the day of the week, time in the term or point in the year.

THE HYPOTHESIS

Another style of 'What happens when?' question is the hypothesis. The hypothesis is used in academic research. Rather than posing a question, the researcher makes a statement that they intend to prove or disprove. For example, 'Early understanding of phonics makes a positive impact on the progress pupils make in art.' The hypothesis can be useful in defining the viewpoint of the researcher; however, it does come with some difficulties as a tool for research. In making the hypothesis, the researcher can bring their own bias to the research. The teaching assistant researching the behaviour of their autistic student in maths lessons could make the hypothesis that 'The mood in which the autistic student enters the class impacts on the escalation of misbehaviour during the lesson.'

In stating the hypothesis, there is a danger of pre-empting the research outcomes and guiding the evidence produced to affirm the hypothesis. The researcher may try too hard to draw out evidence that affirms their hypothesis that the student's misbehaviour is simply linked to their mood on entering the maths lesson. This may be a contributing factor to the student's misbehaviour, but there is a risk that the researcher might wrongly conclude that it is the only cause of the misbehaviour. Caution, therefore, must be held by the researcher in forming a hypothesis as it can narrow the researcher's field of vision or inadvertently lead them to draw unproven conclusions.

THE NULL HYPOTHESIS

In order to counteract the potential bias in the hypothesis, you may choose to use the null hypothesis. This is common in scientific research. While a hypothesis asks the researcher to consider the link between two factors, a null hypothesis states there is not a link. The researcher therefore challenges themselves to disprove their own hypothesis or idea. An example of the null hypothesis, taking the hypothesis posed above, would be: 'The mood in which the autistic student enters the class has no impact on the escalation of misbehaviour during the lesson.'

In this example, while the researcher is attempting to prove the positive link between the student's mood on entering the maths lesson and their behaviour within the lesson, the null hypothesis urges the researcher to seek for evidence that disproves their own assumptions. This is a powerful tool for the researcher as it challenges the potential bias in their research. If the researcher disproves their null hypothesis then their assertion is more likely to be the case.

What is related to what?

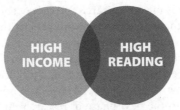

The 'What is related to what?' question considers relationships, or correlation, between differing factors. A research question may consider, 'What is the relationship between low-income families and ability in reading?' It may also be relevant to add a third factor into the question by asking, 'What is the relationship between low-income families, ability in reading and school attendance?' Considered visually, these questions can be represented by a Venn diagram

In our example, the teaching assistant may ask, 'What is the relationship between the student's mood on entering the maths lesson and the misbehaviour observed during the lesson?'

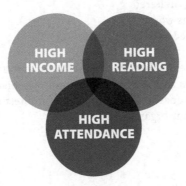

Bringing a third dimension to the question, the researcher could ask, 'What is the relationship between mood on entering the maths lesson, misbehaviour during the lesson and ability to recall key facts learnt in the lesson?' In considering a third dimension, the researcher may discover more or deeper correlations.

Finding the right question

Selecting the style of question for your research will help guide you to a meaningful research question that will become the starting point for your research. In defining the question, you will start to crystallise your thinking around your chosen research issue. The question becomes a hook upon which your research hangs. If properly crafted, the question can also become a simple statement about the body of your research and support both the research project and the methodology that will follow. For this reason, the question at this stage must remain fluid. Availability bias (Kahneman, 2011), an assumption that 'what you see is all there is', could encourage you to think at this stage that you have formed the perfect research question. Be cautious, and keep in mind that you don't yet know what you don't know. It is now important that, as a researcher, you move to the next phase of research: to review what is known about the issue embedded in your research question.

 **Key messages from step 2
'Build a question to answer the issue'**

- Refine your issue into a helpful and purposeful **research question**.
- Consider which of the four styles of questions best suits the research study:

  1. **What's the situation?**
  2. **What's going on here?**
  3. **What happens when?**
  4. **What is related to what?**

- Look out for potential **bias in the questions**, and try not to devise a research question that simply affirms your own bias.
- Build a research question that would be of **interest to both you and others** within your organisation.

Step 3: Review what is known about the issue

Once you have defined your research question, it is time to move on to discover what is already known in this area. Research comes more naturally to teachers in their early careers as they return to practice learnt while at university. For many school staff, however, this may not be a natural step, and some may need guidance in how to review relevant literature and information about their issue.

If your research question is to have meaning and purpose in your organisation then you need to find out how your research question, or issues relating to it, has been raised by others. This will help you to deepen your understanding of the issues that orbit your research question and will help you to refine your question. During this step of the Research Cycle, you may learn about difficulties others had in researching in this area or you may confirm that there has been limited research around your issue. This step is really important but it is one that the researcher in school often omits as they are keen to get going on their research methodology. It is important to slow down and reach out to as many sources of information relating to your research question as possible. As a researcher, you need patience, time and talk. Patience, as you don't want to rush headlong into planning your research methodology before you know what you are doing. Time, as you will need to fit your review into your busy working week. Talk, as you will need to talk to your research coach about the issues that arise from your review of what is known. All this builds what Dimmock (2019) refers to as a 'professional learning community' where a school creates the space where patience, time and talk rests.

Professional learning communities and research buddies

I had the privilege of visiting Singapore in 2019 with a group of ten school leaders to undertake research for the British Council. The research took us into the Singaporean education system, where we met with the Singaporean Ministry of Education and the National Institute of Education – the country's initial teacher training university. We also visited primary and secondary schools and tertiary colleges. During the visit to schools, I attended a professional learning community discussion. During these discussions, teachers were encouraged to engage in research-informed projects and were given time during their school week to meet and discuss their research with one another. Building a culture where research is valued and time is given to staff helped build a professional learning community (Hairon and Dimmock, 2012).

The direction to create the professional learning communities came from the Ministry of Education and is supported and embedded in schools. The professional learning communities also operate across schools, empowering teachers to work beyond their own organisation. The professional learning communities in Singapore, however, focus only on supporting teaching staff. It is my view that to create a professional learning community in school, we must involve all staff. If we are to create a genuine culture of research in our schools, then we should include all staff who work therein. By involving all staff in research practice, an important message is delivered across the culture of the school: we value the voice of all our staff. When I meet with school leaders developing a culture of research in their school, it is often the case that this culture remains exclusively in the purview of teaching staff. We must break down the barriers of exclusivity and support all our staff in becoming researchers. In my schools, there are no limits to who is seen as a researcher. I encourage teachers, teaching assistants, administrative, catering and estates staff to engage in research-informed practice. Building a culture of research-informed practice pervades all we do and empowers staff to innovate, building mutual understanding across the organisation.

Taking the concept of the professional learning community, I have introduced 'research buddies' across my trust. I begin by drawing together the research questions from staff across the trust into broad themes and then produce a bubble map of names. Staff are then encouraged to link with others with similar research themes across the trust as their research buddy. Research buddies then share relevant information about what they have found at step 3 of the Research Cycle. Research buddies can also support one another as they refine their research question at step 4 of the Research Cycle and beyond. In building a culture where researchers support researchers within your organisation, staff become increasingly informed and strengthen their research practice.

Speak with colleagues

One powerful way of deepening a researcher's understanding of their research area is to introduce them to a colleague who has a knowledge base or experience in their field of research. A teacher researching the impact of their teaching strategies on autistic pupils could be signposted to speak with their special educational needs coordinator (SENCo) to deepen their understanding of autism. Widening this further, the researcher could be introduced to a SENCo at a neighbouring school or a teacher from a school specialising in support for autistic pupils. This offers a simple but informative way for the researcher to deepen their understanding of their area of research.

Before heading into the research field to talk with colleagues, think about what you want to get out of the conversation. It is helpful to prepare some key questions to ask. Forming questions both helps refine the purpose of the conversation and helps you to think about what you may not yet know on the subject. A site manager in one of my schools was new to post and his initial research question was 'What systems are effective in building an efficient and cohesive cleaning team?' He was tasked with visiting a well-established site manager in a neighbouring school and went armed with a range of key questions to help him unpack the roles and responsibilities in order to compare these to his own practice. Questions included:

- How do you structure your cleaning team and why have you chosen to do this?
- What are the things you are most pleased with regarding your cleaning team that support them in being efficient and cohesive?
- Do you have any frustrations with the cleaning team that get in the way of an efficient and cohesive team?
- Have things gone wrong with your team and what did you do to rectify this?
- When things go wrong, how do you communicate difficult messages to your team?
- How do you celebrate success within your cleaning team?
- What would your cleaners say are the best or worst things about working in the team?
- If you could change one thing about your team to make them more efficient and cohesive, what would that be?

The focus of the questions allowed the site manager to gain a perspective of how a different organisation had approached the efficiencies in cleaning he was grappling with in his own school. This led to the adaptation of the site manager's research question to then trial and review a new approach to the cleaning structures within his own school.

It is worth noting that speaking with colleagues within your own organisation and beyond has both benefits and difficulties. Benefits include broadening your understanding of the research field. The conversations can forge positive relationships within and beyond your organisation and can also help in increasing your awareness of differing practice relating to your field of study that is not commonplace in your own organisation. Conversations in other organisations may also introduce the researcher to opposing ideologies or practice that can be a healthy challenge to their own bias around the field of study. As a researcher, you need to be prepared for such eventualities and be open to accept what is said to you and hold your own assumptions lightly.

But what of the difficulties you face when speaking with colleagues within and beyond your organisation? When talking to colleagues within your own organisation, there is a danger that you will have limited experience or that the conversation may be too parochial. This could narrow your field of study and lead you to miss the potential broadening of practice as a result of your own research. Or you may have a conversation with another organisation and, without understanding the context, return with ideas that oppose your own organisation's ideals, causing potential conflict in the ranks. Difficulties such as these should be noted, but do not limit the value of speaking with colleagues from beyond your own organisation. As a researcher, it is inspiring to work within an organisational culture that is outward-facing, open to research and welcomes challenge at every level – and worth striving for.

While there are practicalities in engaging with colleagues from different countries and educational jurisdictions, an international perspective can broaden the researcher's understanding of their field of research. It may be impractical to undertake an international visit, but learning about your research field from a colleague who works in a different culture or country can be fascinating. This could be through discussions across educational jurisdictions: for example, a teacher working in England, researching the impact of statutory testing on 11-year-old children, may be interested in speaking with colleagues across the border in Wales or Scotland. Equally, the researcher or their coach may have links with teachers in other countries that would be willing to speak to them to broaden their awareness of the field of study. Video conferencing gives you the ability to cross borders without the need to travel, building an international element to your research work without leaving the comfort of your own room.

The final opportunity that presents itself to the researcher is to engage in discussions with those beyond the profession. One of my curriculum leaders devised the following research question: 'How do I make learning feel irresistible to our most disengaged pupils?' Working with Nick Hind, an education consultant, we sent him to meet with a hotelier in Bournemouth who had created a chocolate-themed boutique hotel. This visit allowed the teacher to develop an understanding of how the hotelier had worked beyond convention to create a business that was 'irresistible' to its clients. This led to the curriculum leader deepening their own strategic thinking when they returned to school. The curriculum leader worked with their team to trial a range of initiatives that gave disengaged students a view of the curriculum beyond the school. As an example, a group of year 6 pupils worked with the manager of a local tea shop to set up and run their own tea room in school for one week. Parents and members of the local community were invited into the school to experience the tea room. This project connected pupils to their local community, gave purpose to their learning and impacted positively on outcomes across the curriculum for the group of disengaged pupils. In drawing from conversations beyond teaching, the researcher becomes increasingly open to using their research to challenge their own understanding and challenge convention within their own school.

Books

Books offer a great resource for the researcher. The research coach can support the researcher to find books, or chapters within books, that link to their field of research. A curated suggestion of a book can guide you to an expert in your field of study that can help crystallise your research question. Books can also lead to further reading through the use of citations and bibliographies. As books have a high level of scrutiny from the publisher before going to print, they are often a more refined source of information than free and online publishing sources. Because of the time taken to publish, however, books can become dated quickly, particularly if the current educational climate is swiftly evolving. Another cautionary point relating to books is that as they are often written by one author – and I need to be cautious here as the author of this book – the content can easily become biased with the author's viewpoint. When approaching a book, you need to be aware of bias in the materials you read and to constantly ask yourself, 'I can see what the author thinks, but what do I think about this?'

A powerful way of finding a great book to read is through recommendation. While you can search for books on given themes, it is always helpful to find a colleague who has read a book and reviewed its impact. In my schools we have a 'virtual bookshelf'. The virtual bookshelf is a database of professional books that I and other staff have read with a very brief synopsis about how the book has inspired the reader. The more books that are added to the virtual bookshelf, the wider the range of research issues that are presented to our researchers across the organisation. What's more, the virtual bookshelf tells the researcher who owns the book. This can connect the researcher with someone in their organisation who has an interest or understanding about their research question. This may be someone the researcher could speak with in order to find out what is known about their research issue.

Journals

Journals provide a rich source of evidence to help deepen a researcher's knowledge of what is known in their field of study. Journals are varied and offer different levels of complexity, so tread carefully here as a complex academic journal can be intimidating to read if you are not used to this style of writing. Some journals are more accessible than others, such as the Chartered College of Teaching's *Impact* journal, which is structured in an action research style and whose articles are written by both school practitioners and academics.

Many journal articles follow a systematic pattern and it is helpful to understand the structure if you are to get the most from the article. The first step is to consider the choice of journal. Talk to colleagues as you may find there is someone in your organisation who is aware of helpful journals that link to your research question. Another really helpful tool is Google Scholar, which is a research-specific search engine. Google Scholar searches for scholarly literature and allows the researcher to explore related works, citations, authors and publications. The next challenge is to help the researcher navigate the structure of a journal article.

Journal articles often follow a set pattern. Understanding the various elements of a journal article can enable you to identify the parts of the article that will help deepen your understanding of your own field of study. The article may also guide you to other relevant research and give valuable ideas about the methodology you could use to answer your research question. Here are ten simple steps for navigating a journal article:

Consider the journal article title. This will tell you the field of study and the journal in which the article was published. Some journals are highly thought of and as a result will have strong quality assurance attached to the publication of articles. Other journals may have less stringent quality assurance. Read any article, but be critical about what is read. (I will explore critical thinking more deeply later in this chapter.)

Check whether the journal article has been peer-reviewed. A peer-reviewed article has been written by an expert in the field of study and then reviewed by several other experts in this field before being published in a journal. This is helpful to know when reading an article as it increases the validity of the research. However, caution must be held for any bias in these articles as peer reviewers may all hold a similar perspective on the field of study.

Where has the research taken place? This is important to understand as the findings of research undertaken in secondary schools, for example, may be different from similar research undertaken in primary schools. Alternatively, research undertaken in a different country or context may also be subject to cultural differences when comparing with work in your own organisation.

Read the abstract. The abstract is an initial summary of the research article. This is a great place to start to decide how relevant the article is likely to be to your field of study. The structure of the abstract also gives you an example of how you can write a synopsis of your own research as it unfolds.

Think about the resources used in the materials section. In this section, the researcher will often talk about resources they used in the study. The research may use a specific survey or questionnaire that could be replicated to allow you to test out the research in your own context, providing a comparative study as a research project. This may be particularly helpful if you have formed a 'What happens when?' style research question.

Consider the research design. In this section, the researcher will speak about how they conducted the study. In particular, look out for the numbers of participants in the study. If there is a large number of participants, this may suggest the study has a high degree of validity. If there are only a few participants, this may suggest a weaker validity to the findings. Again, you need to encourage your researcher to be critical and question the validity of the research methodology. Equally, the design can give you some helpful pointers to direct your methodology to answer your research question.

Consider the research procedure. In the procedure section, the researcher will talk about how the study took place and what the steps were in setting up the study.

Consider how the results inform the discussion. In this section, the researcher will present their findings and apply them to a wider context.

This will guide you to clues on the significance of the data. Researchers use something called the 'p-value'. The p-value describes how likely it is that the findings of the study are random and therefore not attributable to the causes claimed. The lower the p-value, the more noteworthy the findings; a value below 0.05 is considered statistically significant, indicating a less than 5% chance that the results are random. Also relevant is the effect size, usually measured by 'Cohen's d'. This represents how much of an impact can be expected – how much of an improvement you might see in test scores if you use a particular strategy, for example. While a complete understanding of how the p-value and Cohen's d are calculated and interpreted is not necessarily needed in school-based studies, being aware that these indicate the strength of the statistical claim is valuable. I only mention both measures here to ensure that we can demystify their appearance in an academic research article. We therefore need to read this section with confidence to understand how certain the researcher is that their results are significant.

Consider what the research found out in the conclusion. This helps to draw together the entire research project. When reading an article, I often scan the abstract to consider if the article is relevant to my field of study. I then jump to the conclusion to see in more detail what the study has found. If this sounds relevant, I will then dig deeper into the article to try to understand the detail of the research.

What other material is recorded in the references section? This is where the researcher records all their own review of literature. This can lead you to other articles and references that may help to deepen your own understanding linked to the research question.

My top tip for approaching journal articles is to **read the abstract** to test the relevance to your field of study. Then **read the conclusion** to see if the remainder of the article is worthy of a read. **Read the whole article** to seek pointers for your own methodology. Finally, take a look at the **reference section** for further references that could help broaden your understanding of what is known about your research question.

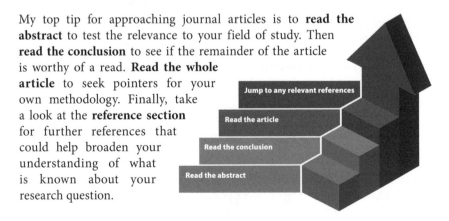

Jump to any relevant references

Read the article

Read the conclusion

Read the abstract

Websites

Websites can be a great source of information for your researcher. If you have devised a research question relating to dyslexia, then websites dedicated to dyslexia awareness can help you gain a broader understanding of your field of study. Websites can also lead you to further resources and materials that could support your study.

It is worth mentioning the limitations that websites can present. As an example, encyclopaedic websites can be a helpful resource in broadening your knowledge base. The difficulty with some such websites, like Wikipedia, is that the information presented can be edited by anybody and can be inaccurate, outdated or just plain incorrect. Conversely, Wikipedia articles can provide a good source of relevant articles as the key information is often cited in a list at the bottom of the article. While you should be encouraged to use websites to support your literature review, you also need to be mindful of their limitations. Again, you need to view this information, as with all evidence, with curious caution.

Professional associations

Professional associations can provide you with a helpful range of information relating to your field of study. Teachers within my schools are given a 'learning ticket' to accompany their research. The learning ticket has a cash value of £150 and can be used to support their research. Teachers often use part of the learning ticket to join a professional association that resonates with their research field. As an example, teachers have joined the Association for Science Education, the Geographical Association and the Chartered College of Teaching. Membership of these associations provides the researcher with a repository of research information that can support their own study.

I run a research group for my early-career teachers. We meet once a term to develop research-informed practice and strengthen research methodology. As an organisation, we sponsor the membership to the Chartered College of Teaching as this provides a wealth of research materials for our fledgling teachers. The materials, journals and research information provided by the organisation can also be adapted to support research for non-teaching colleagues.

The Education Endowment Foundation (EEF) offers a great resource of research undertaken across schools in England (Education Endowment Foundation, 2020). The EEF is a research organisation dedicated to breaking the link between family income and education achievement. The aim of the EEF is to support teachers in raising attainment for disadvantaged pupils. Their website provides the researcher with a range of research studies and their impact on the attainment of pupils. This site can be particularly helpful in introducing curriculum-based staff to current educational practice and tools that have been tested through evidence-informed research.

Conferences and training events

One-off training events can be helpful in building the researcher's knowledge base around their field of study. Conferences, often organised by professional associations, can offer a wider perspective on a given theme and connect you to other researchers in your field of study. Courses and conferences also provide opportunities for the delegates to ask questions of the speakers. This can be really helpful as you can pose questions that relate to your research question, helping you gain a deepening understanding of your research question.

Staff with similar research questions can be grouped together. These staff members can join one another at a conference or training event, providing opportunities for further professional discussions relating to their research questions. This has also led to staff in my schools working together as research buddies on shared research projects as they refine their research questions together into one meaningful study.

Social media

While social media is not everyone's thing, I love it. Social media, through platforms such as Twitter, Facebook, LinkedIn and Instagram, can provide a superb opportunity to connect with colleagues who have complementary or opposing views. Through these and other platforms, you can connect with fellow professionals who comment and link to interesting blogs, articles and sites. Organisations often use social media platforms to connect with their audience and you will find these offer a real-time view of the opinions surrounding a range of issues in schools, whether it is school business management, senior leadership, teaching practice or an insight into the Department for Education – in the UK or beyond.

One aspect of social media that can prove interesting as a researcher is to find a blogger who writes within your field of study. Bloggers often use a range of current issues to form their blog and can lead you to other interesting resources and articles. As with other forms of literature, the discerning researcher needs to be aware of the bias that often appears in blogs, particularly as the blogger is often a single person whose text is unedited by others or who may be sponsored by a wider organisation.

Thinking critically

The Chartered College of Teaching (2020a) offer some useful advice to the researcher on thinking critically about literature. While the advice is centred on teacher research, the principles resonate with literature from the whole range of roles and responsibilities in schools. The advice centres around three points when approaching literature: 'Beware – think fair – take care'. Here are the key points.

BEWARE

When approaching a piece of research literature, you need to beware of claims made by the literature. Claims may have a bad basis. As an example, claims may be too good to be true. This may be rooted in an article that claims a style of practice will lead to 100% of pupils making accelerated progress. Such bold promises can lead to a very blinkered view of a given strategy linked to the researcher's field of study. The Chartered College stress the importance of being wary of claims that are:

- Too good to be true
- Based on faulty logic
- Based on trust alone

Some claims made about research may also appear to be based on sound logic, but watch out for faulty assumptions. This links to the bias called the 'halo effect'. The halo effect comes into play when we meet someone who is extremely enthusiastic about their findings and we want to believe what they are saying because we are drawn into their enthusiasm for the subject matter. Alternatively, we may be enticed into believing that a certain approach to teaching may be highly effective because it is used widely across schools. The enthusiasm for strategies such as Brain Gym at the turn of the century is an example of how what seemed to be a strategy based on sound logic was used to market a product in schools. Brain Gym was sold to schools as a solution to sharpen children's thinking and help to connect the left- and right-hand sides of their brains, giving children greater capacity to think, reason and remember. This was in the context of an explosion of neuroscientific research. Schools lapped this up and introduced Brain Gym style activities and told their pupils that this was helping them to be brighter and learn faster. A number of studies have gone on to debunk these ideas. John Dabell (2020) sums this up: 'Brain Gym is a classic piece of snake oil in education that has been mis-sold to thousands of schools and has been peddled by many in order to cash in on the neuroscience gold rush.'

Another area to be cautious about when considering evidence is the assumption that just because something is associated with a particular outcome, it caused that outcome to occur (Chartered College of Teaching, 2020a). The relationship may be coincidental and you must try to identify whether intervention that is claimed to produce a given outcome is truly the cause.

If something appears too good to be true, it probably is. This is the mantra of the discerning deal hunter. This also applies to the discerning researcher too. As a researcher, you need to beware of negative side effects. The side effects of interventions are rarely reported in educational research. An example of this may be seen in a research study into the benefits of introducing a new method of teaching multiplication. The study may wax lyrical about the positive impact of this study on the pupil's ability to retain their multiplication table facts. However, when you interrogate the practice further, you find that the researcher spent an additional two hours each week teaching tables to their pupils, and while their retention of table facts over time improved, their application of mathematics suffered as little time was afforded to the wider mathematics curriculum during the study. You need to beware of such negative side effects when reading research and when pursuing your own research question.

THINK FAIR
The Chartered College of Teaching then suggest that the researcher should tread with caution when reviewing evidence and 'think fair' (Chartered College of Teaching, 2020a). In thinking fairly about evidence, you should be encouraged to seek out unfair comparisons, unreliable summaries of comparisons and how intervention effects are described.

Unfair comparisons can be seen in the groups selected for study. For example, a teacher studying an intervention in maths may use different groups of pupils in the study such as a previously high-attaining group using the intervention while selecting a previous low-attaining group as the control. The apparent effects of the intervention may reflect the differences in the groups of pupils rather than effects of the intervention itself. To make a study fair, the researcher should, where possible, change only one factor in order to make the test as fair as possible. We teach our primary children about fair tests in science, that by limiting the variables to one and making the test repeatable, the young scientist can attempt to prove a scientific fact. It is just the same with seeking out unfair comparisons: if the test looks at too many variables or would be difficult to repeat, then it is likely to be an unfair comparison.

Unfair comparisons can also be spotted in the assessment of outcomes. Assessment of outcomes that use national testing are meaningful as they use a nationally accredited test. Other outcomes in studies that rely on more subjective assessments, such as comparison of attitudes and feelings, are more open to misinterpretation by the researcher. While subjective outcomes are an important element of research in schools, be cautious here as the researcher may have put some of their own bias into the interpretation of the outcomes.

A final warning about unfair comparisons relates to the inclusion of everyone in the study. It is often the case that in schools, when we are trying to demonstrate positive progress for pupils, we can be tempted to disaggregate a group. With the pressures of national benchmarks, schools can attempt to disaggregate pupils with low attendance when presenting performance data to demonstrate that the pupils whose attendance is strong have performed well. While this gives valuable information to raise questions internally about the progress of pupils whose attendance is high, it falsely represents the performance of the entire cohort. Similar disaggregation can take place in research as the researcher attempts to make an unfair comparison of the impact of their research study by using only those participants who are impacted most by the study, leading to false or biased conclusions.

The second element of thinking fair warns the researcher to watch out for unreliable summary. This may be seen in the under-reporting of relevant research that goes against the researcher's own conclusions. In being alert to this bias in others' work, you will strengthen your own capacity to present multiple perspectives on your own research findings.

The third element of thinking fair asks the researcher to look out for misleading descriptions in the evidence they gather. You should be alert to the use of small study numbers as this may lead the study's author to make unrealistic claims on the significance of their findings. Also, the margin of error, called the 'confidence interval', can give a sense of how clearly the results of a study point to a conclusion. If the confidence interval is wide, then there is a wide range of variation in the results. If the confidence interval is narrow, then the individual results in the study all tell a similar story and the evidence is more likely to be clear.

TAKE CARE

The final step that the Chartered College of Teaching recommend is to 'take care' when approaching the research of others. As a mentor on the Chartered Teacher Programme for the Chartered College, I found that it was this element of the evidence that I spent the most time on with my mentees. There are several elements to ensure you take care in your interpretation of the evidence base. The three key things to consider are as follows:

- What your problem is and what your options are
- Whether the evidence is relevant to your problem and options
- Whether the advantages are better than the disadvantages

This phase of gathering evidence on the field of study helps you to connect what you read with ideas of how you can refine your own research question. As a researcher, you need to understand what the underlying problem is within your own field of study. Consider a teacher with the following research question: 'Do pupils make fewer spelling mistakes when encouraged to write in pencil rather than pen?' Having defined the problem and a potential research question, you can then approach the research of others. By being clear about your research question, your quest for evidence relating to what is already known about your field of study becomes increasingly focused and fruitful.

As a researcher, you also need to be cautious when considering the evidence that at first sight appears to resonate with your own research question or issue. When considering the relevance of the evidence more carefully, it may become clear that the results of the studies or conversation with a colleague in a neighbouring school may not be applicable or transferrable to your own school. As an example, an intervention for homework may be highly successful in one setting that has a high level of engagement from parents, while in your own setting, parental engagement is low.. While unpacking the reasons for this difference can be interesting as a research question, the researcher must remain alert to the impact of context on their research question.

Finally, the Chartered College of Teaching suggest caution over the advantages and disadvantages of evidence on interventions undertaken in school. They state that 'decisions about whether to use an intervention should be informed by the balance between the potential benefits and the potential harms, costs and other advantages and disadvantages of the approach' (Chartered College of Teaching, 2020a). This is to help the researcher recognise that while some research, particularly research celebrating the use of a particular intervention for pupils, can clearly show the benefits of this intervention, there may be unintended consequences of the intervention that have not been either considered or reported. For example, a study into the use of the positive impact on the progress made by pupils in science after the introduction of a new digital assessment system may have neglected to question the negative impact on the workload of teachers in recording accurate data in the system. You should therefore beware of claims that only talk about the advantages of interventions and ignore the potential disadvantages. You must be balanced as a researcher and carefully look for the presence of cognitive bias in the evidence you gather.

THINK FIRST

Another simple system to critically review the research of others uses a simple acronym: 'FIRST'. The acronym stands for funding, investigation, results, subjects and time. The FIRST model offers a simple and helpful framework that encourages caution when approaching research findings, particularly if the research may include bias.

Funding: Consider who funded the research. Is there bias in this relationship? For example, research into the benefits of drinking milk funded by the National Agency for Dairy Farmers may have some degree of bias in its findings.

Investigation: Consider whether the research asked a cause-and-effect 'What happens when?' style question or a 'What's related to what?' correlation style question. The researcher must recognise that correlation isn't causation. For example, crime rates and ice cream consumption both increase in the summer, but that doesn't mean that eating ice cream increases crime rates. It simply means that the two are correlated. Be sure to look for unrealistic correlation claims when reviewing the research findings of others.

Results: You need to think carefully about how the results are presented in the research of others. Your research radar needs to be tuned into considering whether the findings feel objective and trustworthy. Was the journal article peer-reviewed by experts in this field of study or is the article over-opinionated and making sensational claims based on limited data? A good research study is likely to tentatively suggest a finding rather than state findings are certain.

Subjects: When approaching research findings, think about the sample size. Did the research look at a certain group of individuals or a breadth of subjects? Did the research consider a large or small sample size and do the findings reflect and acknowledge the limitations of the sample size? Be suspicious of research over-claiming bold outcomes based on a limited sample size.

Time: Consider how old the research is. While research outcomes can be enduring, some do not stand the test of time. Is the study 20 years old and based on a very different landscape compared with today? Also consider the length of time of the research study as this can make a difference. A longitudinal study of three years may have more validity than a study over three days.

'Beware – think fair – take care' and 'Think FIRST' offer helpful frameworks to check the validity of what is known within the research of others. They will help you to become more discerning when approaching the research of others in step 3 of the Research Cycle as you find out what is known about your research question.

Cognitive bias

Daniel Kahneman gives the following definition of 'heuristic': 'a simple procedure that helps find adequate, though often imperfect, answers to difficult questions' (Kahneman, 2011). If I was to ask you 'How are you feeling right now?', what would your answer be? Would you respond with 'Fine' or 'Never better'? If we are to engage in what Kahneman calls 'slow thinking' as a researcher, we would delve, and ask a question that would elicit a more detailed response. We could encourage the respondent to dig deeper into their response by asking 'Are you equally happy about all aspects of your work life?' This may guide the responder to go beyond their initial and oversimplified response of 'fine', encouraging them to speak more widely about their job role, their relationships with their team leader, their frustrations about appraisal, their joy of teaching music to a group of pupils and so on. The process of providing a simple response to a complex question is called an heuristic response. Research is riddled with heuristic responses and it is important as a researcher that you are aware of the unconscious bias that can form as a result of oversimplified responses to questions. Ensuring your questioning helps you go beyond the heuristic is key in broadening your understanding of your research question.

In his book *Thinking, Fast and Slow*, Kahneman talks of lazy thinking. His book is truly worthy of a read for any researcher considering the effects of cognitive bias on their own research and the research of others. He outlines two systems of thinking. The first system depends on an heuristic response. This lazy thinking allows someone to answer a complex question swiftly without engaging in deep thought. It is in this system of thinking that our cognitive bias runs riot and we come to decisions based on our current thinking or with little thought at all, just like the respondent above who answered 'Fine' when asked 'How are you?' In system 2 thinking, you become alert to the multifaceted threads of thinking and more aware of both your conscious bias and potential for unconscious bias when approaching research. This is why Kahneman calls this form of thinking 'slow thinking': it takes time. In becoming more aware of cognitive bias and recognising this in yourself and in others, you will be better able to move from fast system 1 thinking into deep system 2 thought where the multifaceted threads of your field of study will start to present themselves

I often share the following examples of cognitive bias with my researchers to help them to develop a discerning awareness of their own bias and to spot bias with increasing accuracy in the work of others they encounter. Knowledge of cognitive bias is also valuable to the school leader as a shared understanding of cognitive bias in a senior team opens out the breadth of discussion you can have with one another. I will now draw on some examples of cognitive bias outlined by Kahneman.

AVAILABILITY BIAS – WYSIATI
Availability bias is rooted in our natural response to answering a difficult question. It operates on the assumption that we already know all there is on the topic being discussed. Put in simple terms by Kahneman, he uses the acronym WYSIATI to represent 'What you see is all there is.' This sums up the availability bias in us all: we often assume that we know all there is to be known on a given subject when forming our response rather than taking account of the fact that we may not yet know or understand everything.

An example of availability bias operating in as school can be seen in this scenario. One senior teacher, observing the behaviours in another teacher's class, states, 'Jane's teaching seems to be deteriorating – she has a tough class – she clearly isn't coping well with the pupils.' Jane's team leader has undertaken some lay thinking and their availability bias is blocking them from thinking more deeply about what is not known. When questioned, Jane's work colleague states, 'Jane has changed her teaching strategies recently and is off curriculum as she needs to plug concept gaps for the students who have now entered year 10 after a year 9 where six supply teachers led to poor progression for the students.' Further to this, when Jane is questioned about the issue, the leader finds that Jane has noted the students have poor collaborative skills so has mixed up previously established groupings to help build resilience in the students prior to their accelerated programme for GCSE. While this has unsettled the students in the short term, causing low-level disruption, it is a strategy to support progress in the long term. As you can see, in the assumption that what you see is all there is, Jane's rationale for her classroom management would go unseen. By being cognisant of this cognitive bias, the senior leader is in a far better position to support Jane to get the very best from her students. In research, and in particular when forming the research question or engaging in reviewing what is known about your research issue, you must be alert to the effect of availability bias in both yourself as a researcher and the research and ideas presented by others.

CONFIRMATION BIAS
Confirmation bias is where we seek out only that which confirms what we already know or think. This is seen in the associations we unconsciously make. For example, if you buy a new car, you start to notice that the road is full of drivers of that same car. Of course, the reality is that your choice of new car has no effect on the number of those cars already on the road. Our brains are hardwired to recognise and make sense of patterns and connections. Because of this, we often subconsciously ignore anything that does not support our view of the world and emphasise things that confirm our view. It is important to recognise confirmation bias in the research of others as well as in ourselves as it allows the researcher to move beyond their own realm of understanding or opinion.

So, how does confirmation bias appear in schools and in research? Let us consider the following statement: 'Mrs Jones gets great results in her maths GCSE class by grouping students by gender.' Being aware of confirmation bias, what are the assumptions in the statement? One assumption would be that gender segregation has resulted in achieving great results. A second assumption could be that all students achieve these great results. What also of the quality of teaching delivered by Mrs Jones, who may have a range of interpersonal skills that lead to high engagement for all her pupils. I could go on. Without thinking more deeply about the wider factors the researcher could use this statement to simply confirm what they already think about gender grouping, asserting that gender segregation in the teaching of maths is a positive influence.

SUNK COST FALLACY
Sunk cost fallacy is a cognitive bias that is often seen in education and describes a bias where you continue doing something because you have invested time or money in it. You see this in someone who goes to the theatre to see a play and finds it to be the most tedious experience ever. They reach the interval but

head back to their seat after because they have paid for the ticket and, although they are not enjoying the experience, continue as they don't want to waste the money spent. Taking this bias into the school environment, we may hear a school leader, questioned by their staff on the value of the digital assessment system in place, say, 'We have been using this assessment system for five years. We have invested time and money in the system and it produces super graphs of students' progress.' Then a keen member of the senior team asks, 'Is there a better solution to manage the time our staff are spending entering data into the system? The current assessments on the system are no longer even in line with the new exam board's expectations.' The sunk cost fallacy may lead the school leader to respond by saying, 'I know the system is a bit rubbish and there are much better ones available, but we've spent five years and lots of money integrating this one. We can't change it now.'

Sunk cost fallacy is an unconscious bias in us all and you will find this also in research articles, books and the practice of colleagues. You need to be alert as a researcher to listen for evidence of sunk cost fallacy as this is often used as a key argument for opposing organisational change in schools. As such, research can sometimes be wrongly used to validate the status quo and obstruct the evolution of new practice within our schools.

GROUP BIAS

Group bias is an unconscious bias that relies on the social convention that if all around you agree on something, it must be true. An example of group bias is seen in the story of 'The Emperor's New Clothes', where an emperor is convinced by his aides that his new clothes are invisible to him yet visibly the finest clothes to all around him. As his subjects were all too scared to admit that the emperor was in fact naked, the emperor himself believed what was blatantly not true. Group bias is a powerful and convincing bias and has caused atrocities to take place across the world as groups of people and nations hold biased and unfounded viewpoints.

In the field of research, group bias can be seen where groups of people gather with similar viewpoints. This is often the case on social media where groups of like-minded people meet, forming a bubble of understanding. In order to dispel this bias, a lone voice in the group needs to ask a challenging question: 'But what would others who may disagree with our perspective say, and on what information would their opinions be founded?' This is an important bias for you to challenge as a researcher when gathering evidence relating to your research question.

OVERCONFIDENCE BIAS

'In the modern world, the stupid are certain while the intelligent are full of doubt.'
Bertrand Russell

Find someone who has an absolute view on an issue and you are likely to find overconfidence as a bias. This is also linked to the Dunning-Kruger effect, namely that people with limited knowledge of a subject overestimate how much they know due to their limited knowledge of the subject. It is overconfidence bias that can lead a selection panel to appoint the most enthusiastic candidate and then find they are not capable in the roles and responsibilities of the job. To counter the overconfidence bias, we need to understand the simple principle that the more we know, the more we are aware of how much we don't know. When considering the research outcomes of others or speaking to colleagues about their practice, you need to be alert to potential overconfidence in the evidence presented as it is easy to be swayed by enthusiasm. Bear in mind, if something sounds too good to be true, it usually is.

ANCHORING EFFECT

Numbers can be very convincing in research and can inadvertently sway your thinking. You need to be alert to the dangers of being blinded by big numbers. The anchoring effect (Kahneman, 2011) is a cognitive bias that connects a false validity to research outcomes because the number appears significant. An example of the anchoring effect is seen when shopping and you spot a pair of shoes for £120. You then spot a similar pair for £60 and you immediately feel you have found a bargain. In using your initial reference point of £120, you naturally assume that this is all the information you need and come to the conclusion that £60 is a great price to pay. However, there is a danger of referencing your conclusion to the first or limited piece of information you have, as it may well be that the shoe at £60 is also overpriced and a wider search of other shops would give a much broader picture of the value of these shoes.

Another example of the anchoring effect is seen in the staff room when introducing a new school initiative with colleagues. It is often the voice of caution or dissent that will speak out first in a discussion. The response usually starts with the word 'But…'. The anchoring effect comes into play, and the negative comment becomes the 'anchor' to all other thinking on this issue and the conversation and wider possibilities of a deeper discussion considering all the perspectives available is hampered. As a researcher, there is a danger that you may come across a convincing and compelling argument from a member of staff relating to your research question. If you are convinced by the first strong opinion you meet, you may not deepen your understanding of the wider perspectives of others.

HALO EFFECT

The halo effect is similar in some ways to the overconfidence bias. It depends on an unconscious bias to believe someone who is deeply enthusiastic about their viewpoint or has a track record of performing well. Teachers are more likely to grade a student's essay favourably if the student has a track record of writing well. David Didau puts it in this way when writing about the achievement of boys in English exams: 'Do we expect girls to be more compliant and achieve better than boys in school? Are boys and girls treated differently in school and wider society? We expect girls to be made of sugar and spice and all things nice while boys are unwashed louts. Might we be making it easier for girls to achieve in schools because of the expectation we have of them?' (Didau, 2015).

As you strengthen your capacity to review evidence relating to your research question, you need to draw your attention to the powerful influence of unconscious cognitive bias. In learning more about bias in the work of others, you will become increasingly adept at spotting this bias in yourself and, as such, strengthening your objectivity when engaging in your own research.

Key messages from step 3
'Review what is known about the issue'

- Finding out what is known about an issue is not research, but rather **one of eight important steps in the Research Cycle.**
- In order to build a purposeful and helpful research question, you need to **find out what is already known** about your issue.
- **Professional learning communities** and **research buddies** can be really helpful in connecting with other researchers with similar research questions to share knowledge about what is known about the research question.
- **Speaking to colleagues** who have key knowledge and skills relating to the research question can provide a wealth of helpful context to the research, but be sure to plan the conversation carefully in order to ensure it helps you learn more about the context of your research question.
- Consider **speaking to colleagues beyond your organisation** in order to gain insight into the context of your research question.

- **Books** are a helpful resource to the researcher, but be alert to author bias.
- Approach **journals** that are relevant to your research question, read the abstract, read the conclusion, read the article and follow relevant references to broaden your knowledge of what is known.
- Use **websites** and social media to learn more of what is known about your research question, but be aware of the limitations as some published material will not have been subject to deep scrutiny.
- Consider joining relevant **professional associations**, particularly if they provide access to journals as a resource.
- **Think critically** when approaching what is known about your field of study. Remember to **beware – think fair – take care** or to **think FIRST**.
- Strive to understand the influence of **conscious or unconscious cognitive bias** in both yourself and the work of others.

THE RESEARCH CYCLE
Step 4: Refine the question

Now you have completed the first three steps of the Research Cycle and defined the issue that you would like to study, built a research question to answer your issue and reviewed what is already known in this field of study, it is time to go back to your original research question. One of the greatest frustrations I encounter when reviewing research outcomes with my staff occurs when the researcher reaches the end of their Research Cycle and realises they have asked the wrong research question. With hindsight, if the researcher had taken the time to refine their research question, they may have gained a more fruitful outcome from their endeavours. While future sight is not possible, hindsight can teach us a valuable lesson in the research journey.

Once you have gained an understanding of what is known about your research issue, it is time to talk to your research coach or research buddy about what you now know and whether you need to refine your original research question. You need to reason through, with the knowledge of what you now know about your research issue, what you hope to investigate and the relevance of this to your work or the work of pupils or colleagues in your organisation. This coaching conversation will help you to crystallise your thinking and affirm that your research question is both relevant to your role and purposeful for the organisation.

The research question helps you to start with the end in mind. This concept, explored by Will Ryan in his book *Leadership With a Moral Purpose* (Ryan, 2008), encourages the researcher to craft their research question in a way that guides them to their research end point. At this stage, you must refine your question, while keeping an open mind to your potential conscious or unconscious cognitive bias. A research coach or research buddy is really helpful at this stage as they can ask key questions to tease out any bias in your thinking. If you don't have a colleague who can act in these roles, find a trusted colleague who would be willing to listen to your reasoning in formulating your research question and offer critique.

I had the privilege of inviting Will to speak to a group of headteachers. Will told the story of Roseto, a small town in Pennsylvania. In the mid 20th century, it was populated by a predominantly Italian community. A local doctor noted that from 1954 to 1961 there were almost no heart attacks in the men of the town when compared to the neighbouring town of Bangor. The doctor spoke with Dr Stewart Wolf, then head of medicine at the University of Oklahoma, who looked into this phenomenon. Initial hypotheses were that the small community in Roseto had brought to their American town the rich Italian diet of pasta and fresh vegetables and that this was the root to the good health seen in the town. However, this was not the case, and as the researcher engaged in his work, he found the men of Roseto drinking wine, smoking unfiltered tobacco, and eating an American diet of meatballs and sausages rather than the Mediterranean diet. Puzzled by this, Dr Wolf refined his research question to consider wider factors affecting the low rate of heart attacks seen in the town. As the study evolved, one factor appeared to have a significant effect on the health of the town. Dr Wolf found that the Rosetans had brought from their native Italy a strong culture of community. The town priest worked hard to encourage community events. People in the town spent time with one another, laughed with one another, lived with one another. So it appeared that it was not diet, as originally thought, but rather community that had created the 'Roseto effect'.

Just like Dr Wolf, as a researcher, you may have a clear research question. While Dr Wolf started his research with the question, 'How does diet affect the occurrence of heart attacks in men?', through his review of what is known and wider study, his research question was refined to help answer the question, 'What is the cause of low heart attack rates in men in Roseto?' In refining the question, the researcher is led to the end point that can broaden what is known about an issue or field of study. You must be open to this refinement at step 4 in the Research Cycle, but also open to jumping back to this step at any point in the Research Cycle to ensure your research remains relevant and purposeful to both you and your organisation.

A final point to make relates to the cognitive bias of sunk cost fallacy. After engaging in step 3 of the Research Cycle, you may have new and relevant knowledge that leads you to realise your research issue or question is no longer purposeful to pursue. Sunk cost fallacy could lead you to hold on tight to the original issue or research question as you have put so much thought and time into this and don't want to see that go to waste. A research coach is invaluable at this point, as they can encourage you to understand that because of your new knowledge gained at step 3 of the Research Cycle, you may feel your original field of research has little relevance. If this is the case, you need to consider returning to step 1 to try to re-define your issue in light of what you now know. It is far better at this point to move back a step or two in the Research Cycle than for you to blindly pursue a research question that will not be helpful to your professional roles and responsibilities.

 ## Key messages from step 4 'Refine the question'

- Bring your knowledge of what is already known about your research issue to **look afresh** at the research question formed in step 1 of the Research Cycle.
- Ensure the original research question is **still relevant** and will lead you to find out something new about your practice or the practice of others.
- Consider the **end point** of research and confirm that the research question will help you to this end.
- Ask again: is the research question relevant to your **roles and responsibilities**?
- Based on the new knowledge discovered at step 3, don't be afraid to jump back to step 1 or step 2 of the Research Cycle to ensure the issue is clearly defined and the **research question is purposeful** for you and your organisation.

Step 5: Select the research methodology

By step 5 of the Research Cycle, you have considered and refined your research question, building a broadening understanding of your research issue. It is now time to think about the most helpful research methodology to answer your research question. You need to develop an awareness of the range of research methods available to you in order to select the best method, or methods, to explore your research question.

In pursuing your research methodology, you can choose to collect data through a single research method, or combine a range of research methods. Let us start with a review of the theory behind research methodology. This will help you to define the type of methodology that will help to answer your research question. We will then move on to some practical examples of research methods that you can use to build helpful data that informs your research, readying you for the next step in the Research Cycle.

Quantitative and qualitative research

The terms 'quantitative research' and 'qualitative research' can befuddle staff in school. It is important that you understand the difference and value in each. Put in the simplest of terms, quantitative research uses numbers while qualitative research does not. One misconception is that quantitative research, dealing with numbers, gives the researcher stronger data to interpret than qualitative. This is not the case. There is value in both qualitative and quantitative data, provided the data gained helps you answer your research question.

Quantitative research looks at measurable, or quantifiable, variations relating to the research question, recorded by numbers. An example of this would be seen in a research question asking, 'What is the effect of a new reading intervention on the progress in reading age of a group of pupils with a below average reading age?' The quantitative measure could be to assess the reading age of the subjects in the group at the start of the intervention and then again at the end of the intervention. The change in reading age compared with that of a similar control group of pupils not receiving the intervention could then be numerically compared. This is a technique often used by the EEF (Education Endowment Foundation, 2020) in their research and can be a helpful resource if you are considering the impact of an intervention as a research focus.

Qualitative research looks at variations relating to the research question that cannot be measured by numbers. Qualitative research can include data collected by observing and participating in regular activities. Qualitative data can be captured by a team leader using a new method of coaching to improve productivity in their office team. The team leader, as a researcher, collects data through words or pictures; this may be through conversations, questionnaires, observation and video. Consider a team leader asking the research question, 'Does group coaching strengthen the productivity of administrative tasks in the office team?' The researcher undertakes an interview with each member of the team before and after the group coaching sessions are introduced to help to draw comparisons in the office staff's perception of their productivity as a result of the group coaching sessions. The researcher then interviews staff outside the office team to look for any correlation between their responses and those of the office team in order to understand whether any changes in productivity are also felt by the wider organisation. Qualitative research often considers the participants' perceptions, their opinions, beliefs, actions and attitudes. At first sight, qualitative research can be more complex for the researcher to interpret; however, the information gained from the data collected can provide a rich evidence base to help answer the research question.

While quantitative and qualitative approaches differ, they can both be used within the research methodology. Going back to the research question 'What is the effect of a new reading intervention on the progress in reading age of pupils with a below average reading age?', our researcher can take a quantitative approach and collect reading ages at the start and end of the intervention to see if the intervention has effected a change in the rate of progress in reading. The researcher may also decide on a qualitative approach and observe the pupils' confidence or enjoyment in reading, drawing on wider perspectives on the intervention through analysis of the qualitative data alongside the quantitative data. Quantitative and qualitative approaches to research can therefore be used as distinct approaches or as a complementary approach.

Types of research methodology
LONGITUDINAL RESEARCH

Longitudinal research looks at how things change over time. The researcher collects data on the same subject over a number of periods of time. In limiting the variables in the study, the researcher may choose to track one student or a small group of students across the year, reviewing them at different points in time. An example of a longitudinal study is seen in a research question that asks, 'How do weekly counselling sessions impact on students' behaviour in class?', as the researcher can observe how the counselling sessions affect the students in their study over time.

SINGLE STUDY RESEARCH

Single study research considers only one participant. The researcher examines one variable at a baseline stage and examines how this variable changes over time intervals as an intervention is introduced. Observations can take place over a period of rapid learning or through a more longitudinal study over many weeks or months. Single study research can be used to answer the research question, 'How does a summer-born boy's attention span change over time?'

A researcher might be considering the question, 'How does individual coaching impact on the motivation for a year 11 reluctant writer?' The researcher focuses on the student's attitudes towards writing and ability to write across a range of subjects throughout an academic year. The researcher may choose to interview the student and teachers and consider written work produced at set points in the year. This enables the researcher to gain a broad range of data relating to the student's motivation to write across the year that will help the researcher to refine their future practice.

Single study research has a sample size of one, so can have limited efficacy; however, it does allow the researcher to make detailed observations on their subject. Single study research can be used with 'What's the situation?' style research questions. The single study method helps the researcher to gain an understanding of an element of their practice; in the example above, the researcher gained an understanding of how the student's attitude towards writing changed over time as a result of coaching. Single study research is a helpful model to use if you are a researcher in your first Research Cycle as it allows you to focus intently on your subject and learn about recording clear and accurate observations that inform your research.

MICROGENETIC RESEARCH

Microgenetic research is a form of study where the subject is observed during a period of rapid learning or change. It is used in cognitive development research to note incremental changes over a short time period, such as when a student is learning and mastering a new skill within a single lesson or sequence of lessons. Microgenetic research can be used to answer the research question, 'Why do some children acquire the ability to sequence the alphabet swiftly?' In this microgenetic research, the researcher observes the child in the process of learning the alphabetic code and attempts to draw on the key incremental changes in this process that supports the child's learning. This may be the way the child applies the code in their play, recognises letter shapes in books read, draws letter shapes and letter sequences in their artwork etc. In understanding these steps in a child who swiftly assimilates the learning, the researcher can then consider why this is not the case in other children.

The microgenetic method helps the researcher to gain an understanding of the incremental steps involved in a time of rapid change. This is like slowing down time in order to see the changes that take place – changes that would normally be missed as the change is so rapid – allowing the researcher to notice what is often unseen or observed during a period of rapid learning with increased clarity.

CROSS-SECTIONAL RESEARCH

Cross-sectional research, unlike longitudinal research, collects data on students of different ages or developmental levels at the same time. The researcher can then compare the results of students in these different year groups to help draw conclusions about the similarities and differences they observe. An example of cross-sectional research can be seen in answering the research question, 'How does confidence in music composition change over time?' While the researcher could spend several years tracking a group of pupils studying music from nursery to A level in a single study research method, this is often not practical in schools as it would take such a long time to gather the data required to answer the research question. Using cross-sectional research, the researcher can sample a group of pupils from nursery through to A level in an all-through school with an interview, observation or questionnaire in order to gather data on the confidence in music composition by students in each year group. The researcher is then able to compare the data of students in these different year groups to try to answer their research question about developmental differences in pupils' confidence in music composition.

While cross-sectional research provides the researcher with a range of students of differing ages or developmental levels, it does have limitations as a research method. When compared with longitudinal research, there is potentially more variation in cross-sectional research. Taking the research question above, the variables in this cross-sectional research include the evolving music curriculum, the difference in delivery of music teachers in different year groups and the context of the pupils selected. If you select the cross-sectional research method, you must be open about limitations presented by the variables in the study. Nonetheless, cross-sectional research provides you with the methodology to gain valuable data in a relatively short timescale. The immediacy of data gained from cross-sectional research allows the researcher to use their research findings to inform their practice in a relatively swift iteration of the Research Cycle.

DESIGN EXPERIMENTS

An effective technique to support a research question is to design an experiment that tests it out. Design experiments are particularly helpful if the research question is formed as a hypothesis. The researcher may have a hypothesis that says, 'Maths students work more productively when allowed to listen to certain genres of music.' The researcher then designs an experiment where groups of students are given a mathematical task while listening to various genres of music. The researcher can then gather quantitative data of the tasks completed in a given time or qualitative data, asking the students to reflect on how the music affected their capacity to complete the task – or a combination of both.

The purpose of design experiments is to develop theories about learning. The experiments often involve a new intervention or activity; in the case above, providing music during maths tasks. The design experiment leads to the researcher deciding whether to introduce a new strategy into their teaching to attempt to effect a similar change on a larger scale of students or area of the organisation. Design experiments can also be fluid as the researcher attempts to develop new theoretical perspectives while testing and refining their theories along the way.

The design experiment is helpful in leading the researcher to adapting future strategies or practice. Non-curricular staff in schools can also use design experiments to structure their research. Consider a site manager in school researching the question, 'Can non-bleach-based products clean student toilets as effectively as bleach-based products?' The site manager followed the Research

Cycle and found out what was known about non-bleach-based products on the market and trialled these in different student toilets across the school. The design experiment then asked the students and the cleaning team for their opinions about the cleanliness and smell after using the product for one week. The analysis of data gathered then led to the site manager selecting the most effective product based on effectiveness for the cleaning team and scent for students. Through using the design experiment, the site manager was able to effect a change in practice within the school, leading to a positive change for his team of cleaners and the students.

ACTION RESEARCH

Action research is commonly conducted by classroom teachers who are interested in examining and adapting their own practice. Within my schools, action research is undertaken and used by staff groups in the education, business, estates and welfare teams. The goal of action research is to critically examine one's own practice and then make changes to practice based on the research findings. Action research can be conducted by a single member of staff, or a group of staff working together.

As an example of action research, a group of midday meals staff researched the question, 'What strategies are most effective in creating a calm atmosphere when pupils eat in the school hall?' This project led the team of eight staff to each trial one strategy over the course of the year to test out different ways of improving lunchtime for our pupils and staff. This research inquiry led to the lunch team binding together in shared strategies that impacted positively on the behaviour of our pupils during lunchtime. Action research embodies the very essence of this book and my philosophy to empower staff to become self-aware practitioners. Action research builds a self-improving culture within the school and the Research Cycle can be used as its structure.

THE MOSAIC APPROACH

The mosaic approach (Clark, 2005) was devised as a tool to gain the thoughts and perspectives of young children in research. It is a particularly useful approach when undertaking research with our youngest students in schools as the methodologies used give a voice to participants who are less able to articulate their responses to more formal approaches to research. The mosaic approach encourages the researcher to use more than one research methodology or tool to interrogate the research question. The differing methodologies can test out the validity of data as the methods cross-reference one another.

Clark describes the six elements of the mosaic approach:

- **Multi-method:** the approach recognises the different 'voices' or languages of children.
- **Participatory:** the method treats children as experts and agents in their own lives.
- **Reflexive:** the method includes children, practitioners and parents in reflecting on meanings and addresses the different perspectives of interpretation.
- **Focused on children's lived experiences:** the method can be used for a variety of purposes including looking at lives lived rather than knowledge gained or care received.
- **Embedded into practice:** the method offers a framework for listening that has the potential both to be used as an evaluative tool and to become embedded into early years practice.

With these elements in mind, the mosaic approach becomes a helpful tool to structure research methodology when studying young children. While the mosaic approach was devised as a tool for preschool children, the approach also has merit when working with older students, particularly those who may be reluctant to engage, those with special educational needs or those with English as an additional language. The mosaic approach ultimately gives the researcher a window into the thinking of the students, asking the key question: 'What is it like to be in this place?'

I will now outline some of my favourite research tools that I encourage staff to use in their research practice. These are particularly helpful in the school environment, whether education or business staff. This is not an exhaustive list of research tools; as the saying goes, other research tools are available. These tools can be used in a mosaic approach, with the researcher selecting a range of tools that provide rich data when investigating their research question.

Practical tools for research
Now you understand the theoretical basis of research methodology, it is time to explore the practical tools of research. In helping you to engage in research, the following tools will encourage a creative approach to undertaking research. In training sessions with my staff teams, developing a knowledge of the research tools at their disposal helps them to recognise the playful nature of research – these tools are enjoyable to use and allow the researcher to imprint their own creativity into the research method. These research tools will encourage you to think carefully about what you want to achieve from investigating your research question through

the selection of the tool, or range of tools, that help tease out valuable evidence and data. Matching the right tool to the students or situation is a craft, and one that may take a while to master. Over time, you will become increasingly confident in using a range of these tools through the various iterations of the Research Cycle. Returning to my research analogy of learning the guitar, research tools offer the chords upon which the researcher composes the metaphorical song.

POSTCARDS

It is said that a picture paints a thousand words. It is this very principle that makes postcards valuable research tools for unpacking research questions. The researcher uses a range of postcard-size images as the focus to their study. Images can be from genuine postcards, or a selection of images harvested from magazines or the internet. As an example, a researcher working with a group of teaching assistants may have a range of postcard images including a volcano, mountain stream, skydiver, a comfy chair and a cave. The researcher has posed the research question, 'How does pupil behaviour influence wellbeing in teaching assistants?' The researcher then selects a range of images and places them on the table in front of the teaching assistants. Each teaching assistant is then asked to select a postcard that best represents their feelings when faced with a belligerent pupil, a thankful pupil, an angry pupil, etc. The researcher then interrogates why the teaching assistant has selected this image. This process creates an interesting perspective on the issue relating to the research question and allows the conversation to open up with the teaching assistant about their feelings when faced with different behaviours in children.

You can use also postcards as a tool with young children who are less able to articulate their thoughts and feelings and for those who are reluctant to talk.

Postcards help you to gain a wealth of data from the responses and also from the similarities or differences made in the selection of images across a group.

DIAMOND 9

The diamond 9 research tool encourages your research participants to order their preferences. The diamond 9 can consist of images or statements linked to the research question. For example, a teacher wanted to see whether children in her early years class liked the same activities at home as they tended to select during free play in school. She produced a range of 12 images on postcards and asked the children to rank them in a diamond shape. The children placed their favourite activities at the top of the diamond 9 and those with similar preferences were placed in the middle rows with the least preferred form of play at the bottom. Pictures that were not of interest were discarded, as were any that remained after the diamond 9 was complete.

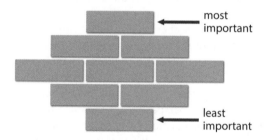

most important

least important

The teacher's research question was, 'Do children favour similar play-based interests in home as they do in school?' The teacher talked to the child throughout the activity and encouraged them to order their preferences. The teacher recorded the final diamond 9 in a photograph, noting the comments made during the discussion with the child as they grappled and reasoned with their choices. The child was then asked to take the images home and repeat the activity with a parent. The class teacher gave the parent a similar narrative to use with the child. Once the new diamond 9 was created, the parent took a photograph. The teacher then compared the two diamond 9 photographs to look for similarities and differences between home and school.

I love this approach with young children as the use of images frees up the research activity and elicits an interesting conversation with the child that can add to the data collected. I have also used the diamond 9 when researching the best design ideas for a new curriculum in school. Rather than images, the postcards had key statements about the curriculum. Statements included

'Knowledge is the most important element of a curriculum' and 'Students learn best when they can see the purpose in what they are learning.' The staff were put in groups and asked to rank the statements with the ones they most connected with at the top and least at the bottom of the diamond 9. Each group was then asked to walk around the room, look at what the other groups had selected and ask questions of one other to clarify their thinking. This process was a powerful tool in exploring the differing perspectives of our teachers and teaching assistants of different subjects within our curriculum. Building this into a research activity, the researcher can then take the responses given by different groups to consider any variance or correlation across teams within the school. Taking the research forward, the same activity can be run with students to see if there is a correlation between what the students and the staff consider the most important elements of the curriculum.

As with the diamond 9 activity with the early years children, the activity with staff built a fascinating bank of data that, when analysed, helped the school to move forward with its curriculum, pedagogy and practice. The research activity also empowered staff, giving them a voice and ownership of the curriculum developments that were formed from the research.

THE TRIANGLE

The triangle approach is one that I have devised to structure research observations or discussions. I use a simple image of a triangle that apportions three questions posed by the researcher to ask what subjects in the study think, feel and do. I explain to the subject that they will be asked questions about what they think, feel and do. When asked about what they think, the subject is encouraged to be factual and try not to talk about their feelings or emotional response to the questions. Once the subject has explored the factual response, their feelings related to their response can be explored in detail during the 'feel' section of the triangle. Finally, the subject is encouraged to focus on their reaction to their thoughts and feelings in the 'do' section of the triangle.

As an example, imagine a researcher investigating the research question, 'Do newly admitted year 7 students feel safe when moving around the school?' The first point of the triangle can be used to ask how the student thinks. The researcher will ask, 'Tell me about where your most and least favourite spaces are around the school. Be descriptive and try not to tell me how this makes you feel – we'll get on to that in a moment.' This asks the student to articulate what they think. The student answers, 'The garden area is best; it's a nice open space with loads of plants. The toilet block is too small – there isn't much space to move around if there are several people in it at once.' The student is asked to provide a factual or rational answer based on what they think. The researcher will then move to the feelings associated with this answer and ask, 'Tell me what you feel when you are in those spaces.' This explores the feelings associated with being in their least and most favourite spaces. The student then shares, 'I love the garden because year 9 aren't allowed in. There's a boy in Year 9 that doesn't like me. I don't like the toilet block because that's where the year 9 lad and his friends wait and they push us about.' The final step of the triangle tool then asks the participant to state what they do as a result of their thoughts and feelings. The researcher asks, 'Tell me what you do as a result of the feelings you have when you think about the toilet block.' The participant then answers, 'I don't go to the toilet in school. This is OK in the morning, but by the end of the afternoon I can be really uncomfortable. I guess that is why I don't concentrate well in history.'

As you can see from this example, the triangle method can give a simple but helpful framework to a research question. The method helped the researcher to define areas in the school where the year 7 pupil felt safe and less safe. As this research project unfolds, the researcher is well positioned to be clear about the thoughts and feelings of a vulnerable group of year 7 students and better plan for their integration into secondary school. While thoughts and feelings are interconnected, thoughts depend on rational observations and feelings on an emotional response to these thoughts. It's a subtle distinction, but by separating these out through the use of the Triangle approach, the researcher gains a deepening insight to the thoughts, feelings and actions of their respondents.

GINGERBREAD MAN

The gingerbread man method uses the image of a gingerbread man as a reference for the research discussion and looks at four key elements in the participant. The method considers the participant's knowledge, skills, values and experience. Similar to the triangle method, the gingerbread man can give the researcher a helpful framework for a research conversation with a participant. As an example of this, a music subject leader in a primary school exploring how teaching assistants support pupils in music lessons starts by asking a teaching assistant, 'What do you know about classical music?' The researcher may then move straight to the experience of the participant and ask, 'Have you ever heard a live classical performance?' The skills of the teaching assistant are then explored through the question, 'Can you play an instrument?' or further to this, 'Have you ever played a brass instrument?' The final element of the gingerbread man will then ask the participant about their values and could be represented by the question, 'What music do you love to listen to and why?' The data gathered from the gingerbread man method helps the researcher to gain an understanding of the underpinning musical knowledge, skills, values and experience of teaching assistants in their school and can then be compared with how this impacts on the effectiveness of the support given to pupils in music lessons.

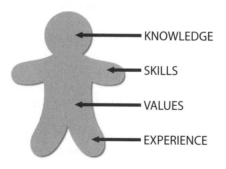

KNOWLEDGE

SKILLS

VALUES

EXPERIENCE

The gingerbread man is a helpful research tool when the subject is a young child as the researcher can gain data through observation. As an example, the researcher in an early years unit could observe a child approach relationships with their peers. The researcher could track that child over the course of a few weeks in a single study research project and note how the knowledge, skills, values and experience gained by the child change the child's approach to their learning or their interactions with their peers. The researcher may choose to focus on how the notion of kindness explored in their curriculum influences the experiential choices made by the subject in their play activities. Alternatively, the researcher may wish to analyse how knowledge learnt in teacher-led learning sessions impacts on the skills used while at play. With the framework of the four elements of the gingerbread man, the researcher is given different lenses through which they can view and gather the data.

HIDDEN VOICES

As a researcher works through the Research Cycle, they devise and refine their research question. They will need to think carefully about the participants in their study. For school staff in curriculum teams, the participants are often students; staff in school business teams may focus more on other adults in the organisation. The 'hidden voices' research tool encourages the researcher to think about those participants in their study that are often not given a voice. For example, returning to our site manager's research question – 'Can non-bleach-based products clean student toilets as effectively as bleach-based products?' – the researcher may choose to involve the team of cleaners in this study, thus thinking about those who would be impacted by the research question but are rarely given a voice. The site manager may then decide to create a sample group of students to give their opinion on the differing products. By involving the students, the site manager has a deeper qualitative evidence base than would be achieved by just involving his cleaning team as participants. While the cleaners focus on the efficiency of the products being tested, the students may focus on unforeseen factors such as the smell left by the product. The hidden voices of the students bring an additional dimension to the research and ultimately a more purposeful outcome for the organisation from the research findings.

As a researcher, it may be relevant to ask yourself if the 'hidden voices' research tool is relevant to your research. A key question here is, 'Are there any individuals or groups that are linked directly or indirectly to my research question who could be drawn into the evidence base for this research project?' If the answer to this question is yes, then you may find this a helpful tool to broaden the evidence base and inform your data analysis.

TAKE A PHOTO

A photograph, or sequence of photographs, can provide a fascinating evidence base for the researcher. Photographs can be used to show the interaction between pupils or the engagement in learning. A photograph can bring a research idea alive and provide the researcher with a clarity of interaction captured in a moment. Coupled with other research tools, the photograph can provide the researcher with a helpful perspective upon which their analysis of data can unfold.

One of my teachers used photographs to record the popularity of activities selected by early years children during their child-initiated play. The teacher, investigating the research question 'Which activities encourage girls to develop gross motor skills?', took a photograph at a given time each day to analyse which activities girls were drawn to in the outside play area. The analysis of this data helped the teacher to reflect on their own practice and build a profile of activities that encouraged girls to develop their gross motor skills more effectively through play.

As with all research, the researcher needs to think carefully about the ethics of their research. In taking and storing photographs of students, the researcher must adhere to the policies and protocols in place in their school, abiding by data protection legislation and safeguarding guidance. It is important to explore the ethics of your research at this step in the Research Cycle. Always speak with your research coach or line manager about the ethics of your research project to ensure this matches your organisation's policies and procedures and maintains appropriate levels of privacy for your participants. I will consider the role of ethics in research in step 5 of the Research Cycle.

VIDEO AND AUDIO RECORDING
Video or audio recording can be used by the researcher to capture data for their study. Video footage can be used by the researcher to carefully review a research subject or event. A researcher considering the research question 'Do year 11 boys or girls ask more questions in maths lessons?' can use a video to focus on their sample group of six boys and girls in the class. Watching the video back, the researcher is able to tally the number of questions asked by the group. The use of the video allows the researcher to observe the sample group without disrupting their usual lesson. If the researcher sat with a clipboard watching the pupils avidly, the pupils may behave uncharacteristically as they become self-conscious because they are being observed. The video footage allows a greater sense of normality in the observation; as such, the data harvested is more likely to reflect normal practice and provide helpful data for the researcher to analyse.

If the research is more dependent on what the subjects say, then an audio recording may best suit. This is another non-invasive method of research that allows the researcher to talk freely to the participants and then analyse what was said after the event. Taking the mosaic approach, the audio recording can be coupled with a diamond 9 activity, giving the researcher additional evidence to record the rationale for the participants' choices in the diamond 9.

As aforementioned, careful thought must be put into the ethics of recording students. Protocols and agreement must be made about where the footage is stored and how long it is retained.

OBSERVATION

Observation in research helps the researcher to have a systematic look into the practice that surrounds their research question. There are two forms of observation: structured and unstructured. Structured observation involves the researcher focusing on particular behaviours in their research subjects. This may include observing a science teacher's use of questioning in class. The researcher notes down the types and frequency of questions asked by the teacher as the lesson progresses. I have used this type of observation when supporting early-career teachers to reflect on their use of questioning in science lessons. I record the time of the observation in the first column, the question asked by the teacher in the second column and the question type in the third column using a question type key. Here is an example of the structured observation grid I used to record my findings:

Time	Question asked	Question type*
0:20	What can you remember about our last lesson?	2 / 4 / 7 / 10
0:50	Who remembers what potential energy is?	2 / 4 / 8 / 10
1:10	What is the definition of potential energy?	2 / 4 / 8 / 10
1:40	Are you sure you are right about that?	3 / 4 / 10

*Question types
1. Observation, 2. Evaluative, 3. Challenges misconception, 4. Affirming/recall, 5. Deepening understanding,
6. Thought provoking, 7. Broad, 8. Narrow, 9. Confused, 10. Clear

This form of observation is called 'frequency count recording' as it records how often the behaviour occurs. In this study into questioning, the researcher is able to use the data to look at patterns of questioning throughout the teacher's lesson. The researcher is also able to see which questions elicit the most responses from pupils, which questions confused pupils, and which questions really challenged the pupils to think deeply. With this data, the researcher can analyse which style of questioning supported the pupils to know more and remember more in their science work. The researcher is then in a position to use their research findings to engage in a wider discussion with the teachers to help refine their practice in use of effective questioning in future science lessons, closing the Research Cycle as teachers adapt and affirm their practice at step 8.

The second form of observation is unstructured observation. An example of unstructured observation is seen in tracking an individual pupil in the early years. A researcher may be interested in gaining an understanding about the difference in play between children from disadvantaged backgrounds and those not from disadvantaged backgrounds. The researcher selects a time period in the day when they observe the child or children, tracking their interactions with peers, their interactions with adults, their choices in activities, their attention to task, their level of engagement and their happiness. This form of observation helps the researcher to record data relating to how the child interacts with their environment and peers. The unstructured observation can allow the researcher to notice something they were not expecting to see in their research, broadening their understanding of their practice and deepening the potential analysis of data. Unstructured observations can provide the researcher with a vast array of data that is difficult to unpack; however, as the analysis progresses at step 6 of the Research Cycle, correlations start to appear in the evidence base that can form interesting and insightful conclusions.

QUESTIONNAIRE

A questionnaire is a great way of gaining an insight into how your research subjects think. A well-crafted questionnaire can provide a rich set of data for the researcher to analyse in support of their research question. Questionnaires, if poorly crafted, can encourage unconscious bias to the responses given. Questions have the potential to be misunderstood by the respondent and this can lead to answers being misinterpreted.

Questionnaires can ask either open questions that elicit a wide range of responses or closed questions that seek a specific answer. Gary Thomas (2017) outlines five helpful pointers to creating an effective questionnaire:

Keep everything short – Don't make your questionnaire too long. Your respondents are less likely to complete a long questionnaire thoughtfully.

Be clear about what you are asking – Avoid questions that ask for more than one piece of information at a time, such as, 'Do you enjoy reading to yourself as well as to children?' This may lead your respondent to answer the question, 'Do you enjoy reading?', 'Do you enjoy reading to children' or even 'Do you enjoy reading to yourself as much as you enjoy reading to children?'

Be precise – As your respondent's only source of information is the questionnaire, you need to be certain that your questions are precise. Watch out for questions such as 'Do you read for pleasure?' Instead, break the question down into its parts by then asking, 'How often do you read for pleasure?' and providing a choice of options, such as 'more than once a month', 'once a month', etc.

Collect all necessary details – Make sure your questionnaire asks for the right information. This may be the age, gender or role of respondents. A researcher thinking about the viewpoint of staff on a particular initiative may kick themselves after receiving the questionnaire responses when they realise they have not asked for the job role of the respondents. Think carefully about both the questions and the contextual information you need to support your study.

Be aware of prestige bias – This is where the respondent may want to impress you or to appear more knowledgeable about your research issue than they are, so may answer in a way that makes them look good, rather than give a truly honest answer.

Once you have considered these five key pointers, you need to carefully think about the kinds of questions to ask in the questionnaire. Here are a range of question styles for your questionnaire suggested by Gary Thomas (2017).

Dichotomous questions
Dichotomous questions are ones that can only be answered in one of two ways. They are often seen as yes-or-no questions. For example:

Have you ever taught an autistic student?   Yes ☐
                                                   No ☐

The dichotomous question can be really helpful in sorting your respondents into groups. The questions that follow can then analyse similarities and differences in the respondents. In this case, a researcher may be interested in finding out about differing approaches of staff who have prior experience in teaching pupils with autism.

Multiple-choice questions
Multiple-choice questions provide two or more closed responses. This can provide the researcher with a response that they can quantify in their research analysis. For example, a senior leader researching the training needs of teaching assistants to cover a class may ask:

Which of the following subjects would you feel confident delivering as a cover supervision activity? (Tick as many as you like)

Maths   ☐
English   ☐
History   ☐
Science   ☐
Geography   ☐
Music   ☐
Art   ☐
Design Technology   ☐
French   ☐
Religious Education   ☐
Computing   ☐

In designing the questionnaire, the researcher may choose to limit the responses to just three answers (or even just one) per person, say. From this style of question, the researcher can create a graphical representation of the responses of the whole sample group.

Rank order questions

Taking the structure of the multiple-choice question, you may want your respondents to rank their preferences. An example of this is seen in a researcher trying to answer the research question 'What drives GCSE choices in dyslexic boys?' A rank order question could be as follows:

Rank these subjects with your favourite subject as 1 and least favourite 6.

History   _____
Science   _____
Geography   _____
Music   _____
Art   _____
Design Technology   _____

This question may then lead to further questions, perhaps assessing the respondents' confidence in the subjects or their enjoyment of the subjects taught. This allows the researcher to try to bring the different responses together to seek an analytical truth about their research question.

Rating scale questions

Rating scale questions ask the respondents to rate their opinion on a scale. Consider a researcher analysing the effect of training on their team:

After attending the departmental training on marking in maths last term, what impact has this training had on your workload?

Very positive impact ☐
Positive impact ☐
Neutral ☐
Limited impact ☐
No impact ☐

The rating scale question is helpful in defining the mood of your respondents. There are limitations to this and one I often advise researchers to think carefully about is the choice of an even or odd number of responses. In this example the researcher has selected an odd number of responses. This allows the respondent to select the mid-point, or 'neutral' comment. Providing a neutral option runs the risk of nullifying the question: if your respondents all choose to sit on the fence, you won't learn very much. By limiting the responses to an even number, the respondent is forced to think harder and make a judgement about which side of the fence they come down on.

Constant sum method

The constant sum method is a great way to get your respondents thinking as it asks them to quantify the value of their responses to the question. You give your respondents 100 points to allocate to any category in the question. The respondent may choose to allocate 20 points to one response, 34 points to another, 15 to another and so on, based on how important each element is. Here is an example of a constant sum question for a researcher looking into the environment for autistic learners:

What are the most important elements of an autistic-friendly classroom?

Muted colours ☐
Simple displays ☐
Clear routines in place shared with students ☐
Availability of ear defenders ☐
Clear behaviour expectations ☐

Autistic-aware staff	☐
Autistic-aware students	☐

The constant sum method, Thomas suggests, is best undertaken with the researcher present as the researcher can pick up on the strength of feeling in the respondents. The data produced from this style of question also allows a refined quantification of feeling from the respondents that can be picked up further in the analysis of the data.

The researcher can also apply this question to a range of subject groups. For example, the question could be asked of the teachers, teaching assistants, a group of autistic pupils or a group of non-autistic pupils. The data can then be analysed for correlation between differing groups, providing the researcher with a wealth of analysis that can inform their practice.

Matrix or grid questions
Matrix or grid questions give the researcher an opportunity to ask the respondent to quantify their responses to multiple interrelated questions, comparatively assessing a range of different criteria. You need to make sure that the respondent is clear about the scale. The benefit of this method is that the respondent applies their own interpretation of the scale and uses this to standardise their responses across the full set of questions.

Here is an example of a matrix question used in research into teaching assistants' confidence in supporting different mathematical concepts:

How confident are you in supporting children in year 6 with these mathematical concepts?

	Deeply unconfident	unconfident	confident	very confident
Identify common factors, multiples and prime numbers	☐	☐	☐	☐
Divide proper fractions by whole numbers	☐	☐	☐	☐
Use simple formulae	☐	☐	☐	☐

| Convert between miles and kilometres | ☐ | ☐ | ☐ | ☐ |
| Calculate the area of a parallelogram and triangles | ☐ | ☐ | ☐ | ☐ |

Semantic differential scale

The semantic differential scale uses opposite adjectives such as 'fair/unfair'. A seven-point scale is commonly used for the respondent to mark their positioning between the two adjectives, allowing for a more graded response. An example of the semantic differential scale can be seen in the following question:

How would you define your approach to teaching art?

	1	2	3	4	5	6	7	
Practical								Theoretical
2D								3D
Paint								Pencil
Noisy								Calm
Controlled								Loose

The semantic questionnaire also creates interesting discussion points for respondents. I often find that once the researcher has collated the results, it is interesting to present these to the respondents and hold a further discussion as you analyse and interpret the results.

ONLINE SURVEY

Online surveys are a great way of sharing your questionnaire with a wide range of respondents. The online survey can also help in collating the responses as online questionnaire tools often have an integrated analysis function. There are a range of online survey providers such as Survey Monkey, Google Forms or Microsoft Forms. Online surveys, like any form of questionnaire, need to follow the key elements explained above if they are to provide you with helpful data for your research.

Through the use of social media, the researcher can utilise their professional connections. Connections can often provide the researcher with data from a range of organisations, types of school and age ranges. Online surveys can also reach respondents from multiple educational jurisdictions, providing an international element to the research study.

Social media can be used for in-the-moment surveys. Both Facebook and Twitter have polling functionality. A researcher looking into teacher retention could post a simple poll asking teachers to respond to the question, 'Have you thought about leaving the profession in the last six months?' In a matter of minutes, the well-connected researcher may have 50 or more responses. However, a word of caution here would be the unconscious bias that lies in such polls. It is likely, for instance, that the researcher is connected online to mostly like-minded colleagues and, in sending a poll, will receive like-minded responses that may not be representative of a wider sample of respondents.

INTERVIEW
A face-to-face interview gives the researcher a powerful evidence base for their study. While the principles of forming interview questions are similar to those for the formulation of a questionnaire, the interview allows the researcher a far deeper insight to the responses given by their participants. The researcher is able to read body language, enabling them to interpret the respondent's emotions and the subtleties to their responses, both of which can flavour the research evidence.

Body language is a fascinating field of study in itself. I had the privilege of hearing Barbara and Alan Pease speak in the late 1990s about body language, and their book *The Definitive Book of Body Language* (Pease and Pease, 2017) is a great reference point for those interested in exploring the subtleties of body language.

In approaching the interview, you need to think carefully about the questions you want to ask. The questions must help you to answer your research question. Keep your research question in mind when structuring the interview as it is easy to allow questions to form that can detract from the key purpose of your research. Unlike the questionnaire, the interview involves building a relationship between the researcher and the respondent. As such, you need to think about how you will introduce yourself and explain your research question to the respondent. You will need to put the respondent at ease. If the initial questions are too challenging, the respondent may limit their responses.

77

If the questions are too inquisitorial, the respondent may feel threatened. As a researcher, you must build rapport and trust with the respondent to elicit honest and thoughtful answers.

Here are a few points to consider when engaging in an interview.

Before the interview:

- **Prepare** your questions.
- Ensure your questions help you answer your **key research question**.
- **Trial** your questions with a colleague/students outside the research group to check for clarity before using them in the field.
- Ensure your sequence of questions has a **flow** in order to create a logical chronology, helping to build a genuine dialogue with your respondent.
- **Write a rationale** for the interview to share with your participants where relevant.
- Consider whether you are going to record the interview; if so, **check permissions** with the participant.
- If you are interviewing students, **seek permission from school leaders/parents**.
- Think about how you will record **subsidiary questions and responses**, should they arise in the interview.
- Consider the **setting** to ensure distractions are minimised and the participant feels comfortable.

During the interview:

- Explain the **purpose** of the interview to your participant.
- Address the **confidentiality** of the responses and how you intend to use them in your research.
- **Explain the format** of the interview, including how long it is likely to last.
- Ask your participant if they have **any questions about the process.**
- Offer to **share the outcomes** from the study with the participants (if colleagues).
- Keep your poker face on: try to **remain neutral** when note taking; if you appear surprised by or agree with a response, your participant may be influenced by this.
- **Stay on track.** It may be tempting for you or your participant to go on a segue and talk about matters that do not relate to your study. Politely bring the participant back and explain why you have done this.

After the interview

- **Share** relevant research findings with your participants.
- Where relevant, **check your participant is happy with how they have been represented** in the research findings before sharing more widely.

Ethics and permissions

Ethics are defined as the moral principles that govern the conducting of research. Jane Zeni, writing in the journal *Educational Action Research* (Zeni, 2006), provides a helpful ethical checklist for school-based researchers. She states that as classroom researchers, we ask ourselves these key ethical questions when engaging in research activity:

- What are the likely consequences of your research?
- How well do these consequences fit with your own values and priorities?
- If you were a participant, would you want this research to be done?
- What changes might you want to make to help you feel comfortable?

I have built on Zeni's ideas to formulate this ethical checklist to support research methodology at step 5 of the Research Cycle:

Does your research go beyond the usual practice in school and as such require students to answer personal questions about themselves, their family or community?

Which of the research participants have read your research question? Which ones have been informed of the research orally in some detail? Which ones know little or nothing of this project? Explain and justify the decisions behind your answers.

What do your students know of this project? Who told them? What are the risks to them or their families of their knowing (or not knowing) what you write or collect? Explain your decisions.

Who else will read or hear about your research? Will this affect your participants or others' perception of them?

You will inevitably gather more data than you need. Consider why you choose to report some data to a wider audience and why you choose to keep some for your colleagues, your students or yourself. Consider the impact on others in the choices you make about what data you choose to use and what you choose to leave out in your analysis.

How will you store and catalogue your data during and after the study? Who will have access? Should you take special precautions with your notes and other data? Have you checked how this affects the organisation's own policies on data management and data protection?

Will this study evaluate your own effectiveness or a method to which you are committed? How will you protect yourself from the temptation to see what you hope to see? What is your own unconscious bias in your research findings?

How do your school leaders see your work? Is your research under suspicion or is it mandated from the headteacher or senior leaders in a drive for organisational change? Is there protection for your own thoughts, feelings, interpretations? How safe do you feel in your school pursuing this research? How safe do you feel in reporting what you learn to a wider audience?

What data will be contributed by others? Will you be recording case studies, oral histories or other stories that may be considered the property of others? How have you arranged with colleagues or other participants for credit in your manuscript or other recognition?

Who is responsible for the final report? Will school leaders review your report in draft? Will this: (a) improve your accuracy? (b) compromise your candour?

Participants may not agree with part or all of your interpretation. If this is the case, you may revise your views, quote their objections and explain why you maintain your original view, or invite them to state alternative views in an appendix.

Have you decided on anonymity or on full acknowledgement if your study is eventually published? Perhaps you will identify teachers, but use pseudonyms for students. How and when have you negotiated these issues?

Do you need to seek permission from parents, staff or school leaders?

While research in school may not require you to seek full ethical approval in the same way that a postgraduate researcher beyond your organisation would be required to, it is nonetheless an important consideration at step 5 in the Research Cycle. It is vital to think about the value to and potential impact on yourself, your participants and your organisation. Thinking about the ethics of your research will also enable you to keep within the bounds of your organisation's policy and practice relating to safeguarding, data protection and information sharing.

Conclusion of step 5

Selecting the right research methodology is an important step in the Research Cycle. The right research methodology helps you to gather valuable data, enabling you to answer the research question as you analyse the data gathered in the next step of the Research Cycle.

In step 5 of the Research Cycle, you will reflect on the differences between qualitative and quantitative research methods. Staff in schools will likely have had very different educational experiences. Those who have come through an academic pathway will be more open to the theoretical elements of research methodology, while others will have to tread more nimbly through this step. A research coach can play a helpful role at this step in the Research Cycle, supporting you to understand the theoretical approaches to research and selecting your research methodology. Choose your research coach wisely; they will help you as you move through different iterations of the Research Cycle, becoming increasingly confident about the theoretical basis to research methodology and more astute in selecting the research methodology that best fits your research question.

The mosaic approach to research methodology really helps you design meaningful research practice where multiple perspectives are gathered from participants. With a purposeful research focus, a refined research question and awareness of what is known on the subject, you are now ready to carefully select the research methodology that will help to provide a rich data set. Whether you select one research method or a range, you will become increasingly astute at gathering evidence that is meaningful, helping you to answer your research question. The methodology brings your research into focus, providing a deep resonance to others across your organisation and beyond when you are ready to share your research findings at step 7 of the Research Cycle.

Finally, when thinking about the theoretical approach to research methodology and the practical tools that are to be used, you must also remember to think about the ethical issues that arise in your research. This will ensure that potential organisational risks, cognitive bias, relationships with colleagues and the safety of students are considered. Take care to follow step 5 and your research will result in a body of evidence that has integrity, interest and purpose.

 **Key messages from step 5
'Select the research methodology'**

- In its simplest of terms, **quantitative research** uses numbers while **qualitative research** does not.
- **Quantitative and qualitative** approaches to research can be used as distinct approaches or can be combined to provide a rich data set for analysis.
- **Longitudinal research** looks at how variables or research subjects change over time.
- **Microgenetic research** helps you track one research subject over time.
- **Single study research** allows you to focus in detail on one research subject; this is a great starting point for the fledgling researcher.
- **Cross-sectional research** considers students of different ages or developmental levels at the same time. This allows you to gather a wide evidence base in a relatively short time frame.
- **Design experiments** help you to develop theories about practice and learning. As a researcher, you build or design your own practice and test this out on a subject or group in order to inform your own practice.
- **Action research** helps you to critically examine and adapt your own practice in school.
- **The mosaic approach** to research, introduced by Clark (2005), is a method of combining a range of research tools in order to provide valuable data for analysis. The approach was often used with younger children in order to gain an understanding of the child's lived experiences.
- **Postcards** can be used as a research tool to get participants to use images to explore their thinking around the research question.
- The **diamond 9** research tool encourages the respondents to rank images or text in order of interest of preference.
- The **triangle** approach draws out the thoughts, feelings and actions of subjects in the research study.
- The **gingerbread man** method discovers the subject's knowledge, skills, values and experience and considers how these are interrelated.
- The concept of **hidden voices** encourages you to consider anyone in your

organisation that may be linked to your field of research, particularly those whose voices are not often heard.

- **Photographs, video and audio recordings** can be used to provide valuable data for analysis, allowing you to reflect on observations without disrupting the natural flow of the participants.
- Observations can be both **structured** and **unstructured**. Both styles of observation can provide valuable data for analysis.
- **Questionnaires** are a helpful research tool but the questions need to be thought about carefully to ensure the data gathered from them helps in answering the research question. Questionnaires should be **short, clear and precise** and collect the necessary details related to the research question. You also need to be alert to **prestige bias** when analysing the data provided by questionnaires.
- **Online surveys**, like questionnaires, must be structured carefully. They offer a helpful tool for reaching a broad range of respondents.
- **Interviews** must be carefully structured by the researcher with careful preparation before the interview and clear protocols within the interview. The interview is really helpful in building a relationship with the respondents in the research study.
- **Ethics** need to be considered to ensure that the likely **consequences of the research are carefully thought through**. This will enable you to keep within the bounds of the organisation's policy and practice relating to safeguarding, data protection and information sharing.

Step 6: Analyse the findings

Now you have gathered a rich array of data at step 5 of the Research Cycle, it is time to set to the task of analysing the findings. It is likely that you will have collected a wealth of raw data using your chosen research methodology. If you have used a range of research methodologies, your data may include transcripts from discussions or interviews, responses to questionnaires, recordings from class groups, diamond 9 pictures and accompanying notes. You now need to think carefully about deciding which data to analyse. You need to seek out the data that is helpful in answering your research question.

The analysis of findings helps you search for patterns within the data gathered. Patterns within the data may be presented as similarities or differences, common occurrences, abnormalities or points of interest.

Synthesis and analysis

Synthesis is the art of drawing together the many elements of your data to form a conclusion and answer the research question. Synthesis is key to the researcher who has a wide range of data to interpret. Analysis is the art of taking things apart in order to understand them. The researcher may be faced with unpacking a complex issue, and through their research and data analysis, they are able to break it down into its smaller parts, bringing clarity to the analysis.

Both synthesis and analysis have a role to play when interpreting data. As a researcher, you must also ensure you hold your assumptions lightly. In other words, in analysing the data, you need to be tentative when drawing conclusions and recognise what the data can or can't say. A study may find positive effects from an intervention but this does not necessarily mean the results can be replicated elsewhere. For example, an intervention that resulted in accelerated reading progress in a sample group may not have the same effect on all pupils across the school. As a researcher, you need to use words that encourage cautious conclusions and recognise the limitations of what the data may suggest. You should also continue to be aware of your own (conscious or unconscious) bias at this stage as it is very easy to guide the data to affirm your own assumptions.

In order to strengthen your research practice at step 6 of the Research Cycle, let us now explore a range of tools you can use to structure the analysis or synthesis of the data; helping you to make sense of the research narrative that unfolds, leading to clarity in answering your research question.

Analysis of words – the constant comparative method

The first strategy in analysing data is the constant comparative method. This is used when you have collected evidence in words and don't want to convert the data to numbers for further analysis. The constant comparative method of analysis involves reading through the evidence collected and comparing similarities, differences and anomalies in the words. You will need to read the data over and over to compare and contrast in order to seek patterns of information you can analyse.

Thomas (2017) provides a helpful checklist for the researcher analysing written evidence. I have simplified this in these six steps:

1. **Read through** your written data.
2. **Mark up your data**, highlighting points of interest and similarities across the data; make notes about parts you find relevant or interesting.
3. **Draw initial thoughts together** linked to your research question from your first read through.
4. Use your initial thoughts or emerging findings to **reread the data** to seek for further patterns relating to your research question.
5. Make notes of **key patterns** and helpful quotes from the data that can be used to answer your research question.
6. Draw out the **key themes** from your analysis, map these out and illustrate them with the quotes you have highlighted.

These steps help to focus your mind when reviewing words. Be playful in your analysis, writing out transcripts of recordings, annotating them with notes and colours to seek patterns within the words.

Mapping out your findings

Creating a pictorial map of your analysis of written evidence can help you to visualise and spot any patterns in the data. There are a number of ways this can be done. Here are four maps that could support your analysis.

MIND MAPS

I first came across mind maps when lecturing in primary education at Canterbury Christ Church University in the late 1990s. My students were grappling with how to make effective notes and I used the mind maps of Tony Buzan (2009) to help them connect ideas during lectures. This process looked at recording key words, images or ideas and drawing connections to show how these ideas were interrelated. As an example, the idea of effective assessment in primary science is linked to the key content covered in the curriculum, an understanding of what should be known, understood and applied by the pupils and a clear purpose for collecting this assessment information. This written information could be summarised in a mind map, as shown below.

FLOW MAP

David Hyerle (2011) took Buzan's idea of the mind map and applied this to structure a range of 'thinking maps'. These maps can also be really helpful when analysing written data. One is called a 'flow map'.

The flow map helps the researcher to define cause and effect within their research. The researcher will have reviewed the raw data, and if there is a clear series of consequences from their data, this can be recorded in a flow map. As an example, a teacher researching the impact of the introduction of a new memory retention initiative in geography could record their analysis using this template. The teacher's research question is 'Does retrieval practice affect pupils' confidence in geography?' A new element of the strategy is introduced by the teacher each term, and the teacher reflects on the impact this has on the pupils' perceived confidence, recording the element of the strategy introduced and responses of pupils to this practice. By presenting this information on a flow map, the researcher is able to clarify the cause and effect of the new practice they are researching. The flow map produced is shown here.

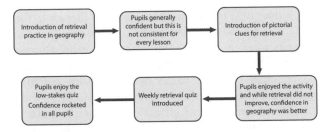

DOUBLE BUBBLE MAP

The 'double bubble map' is another of David Hyerle's creations. It allows the researcher to compare and contrast two things. For example, a researcher may be pursuing the research question 'How does teaching style impact on student learning in history?' The researcher selects two research methods: the triangle and a questionnaire with pupils and staff. In reading through the narratives from the triangle discussion and responses to the questionnaire, the researcher uses the double bubble map to lay out the similarities and differences in the learning of students being taught with a didactic textbook-based approach as opposed to a discussion-based approach. The double bubble could look like this:

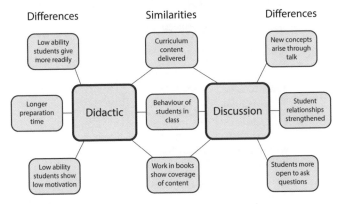

The researcher has used this double bubble to map out the key similarities and differences they have noted in the written data. With this clarity, the researcher is now in a strong position to make sense of the data and draw together their analysis of their key findings.

TREE MAP

David Hyerle also invented the 'tree map'. The purpose of the tree map is to help the researcher classify their findings into key branches or categories. While the tree map does not help the researcher to consider the interconnectivity of their findings, it does help them categorise common threads to their data. An example of this would be seen in a research question like 'What are the most effective strategies to encourage reading at home for my reluctant readers?' The researcher may have used the triangle method as a strategy to speak with students and considered hidden voices by interviewing parents. They may have also produced a questionnaire to survey the pupils in their class and had discussions with colleagues across schools to review thoughts, feelings and actions further. The researcher carefully reads through the evidence base and decides to categorise their findings into three branches of thoughts, actions and feelings using the tree map below. The researcher can then unpack the common themes drawn from the evidence base.

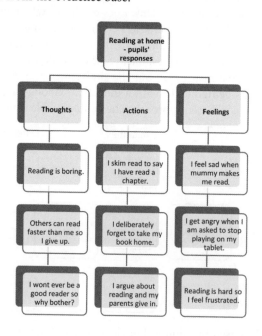

The tree map helps to categorise the data. Taking this example further, the researcher may also seek the parents' views on reading at home. The researcher can now produce a second tree map that explores the data related to the parents' thoughts, actions and feelings. The researcher is now able to compare and contrast the two viewpoints in their research analysis using the two tree maps from pupil and parent responses. With this insight into the different perspectives of pupils and parents, the researcher can use this synthesis of data to reflect on their own practice in order to best support reluctant readers in the future.

Turning words into numbers

In analysing the data gathered, it is sometimes helpful to convert words or images (qualitative data) into numbers (quantitative data). For example, in an interview, the researcher may ask the respondent to give their reason for becoming a teacher. The answers will probably vary across the sample group; however, themes may arise that can be quantified by the researcher and displayed in a coding frame as shown below. Let us say that out of the 30 respondents, the answers fell into four broad categories: a desire to help, a fondness for pupils, job security and career development. The researcher can create a coding frame to help turn the words into numerical data by a simple tally. This data can then be used to present findings and undertake further analysis by the researcher as shown below.

Why did you become a teacher?			
a desire to help	a fondness for pupils	job security	career development
6	12	8	4

Analysis of numbers

As with the evidence gathered as words or images, numerical data requires you to read and reread this data. This process is called 'eyeballing' (Thomas, 2017) and involves the researcher looking at the range of numbers in their findings to search for patterns in similarities, differences and anomalies. To make the eyeballing process easier, you can convert numbers into pictures or graphical representations such as graphs, charts and pictograms. This helps you to spot patterns that you could miss by looking at the numbers alone.

It is easy to become befuddled or threatened with the complexities of statistical analysis. Undertaking complex statistical analysis of your data may be intimidating or cause you to go 'data blind' and become overwhelmed by the data presented to you. Although the complexities of finding statistical variances, frequency distributions, standard deviations and correlation coefficients may be beyond the reach and purpose for many school-based researchers, you need to present your data in a way that allows you to see it in its simplest form. When the data is presented simply, you can use your skills of eyeballing to seek meaning in your analysis.

Here are some pointers to a few methods of graphical representation of numerical data that might help you to eyeball data in order to draw out meaning.

BAR CHART

A bar chart is helpful when the data is in the form of a list or a tally. By representing this information on a bar chart, you can easily spot differences in the data presented. The bar chart works well when the data has a set of variables that can be measured on the horizontal axis compared with one measurement, or frequency, on the vertical axis. An example of this is seen in a set of data that looks at the number of times primary pupils raised their hands to answer a question posed by the teacher in different lessons. Here, the researcher is looking to quantify the data so they can easily see the differences and display these to others in their analysis of the findings.

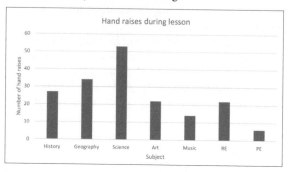

DISTRIBUTION CHART

The distribution chart is similar to the bar chart. Rather than presenting the number of responses in each variable, the distribution chart groups responses into a range. This is particularly helpful when presenting data involving two numerical sets. An example of this is seen in the analysis of data from a study into the relationship between close friendships and wellbeing. One researcher in my school asked the question 'How does friendship group size affect wellbeing during playtime?' They asked pupils about their wellbeing and how many friends they have. The researcher grouped the pupils by their number of friends and took the mean perception of wellbeing for each group. The data was then presented in the distribution chart below.

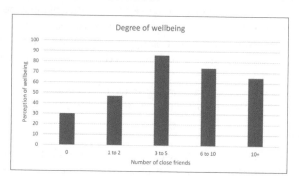

The researcher was able to demonstrate that for their sample group of pupils, the optimum number of close friends was 3 to 5, resulting in the greatest level of wellbeing. The graphical representation helped the researcher to spot the broad picture painted by their data. From this, the researcher is now able to drill down in their wider evidence base to unpack their thinking in the analysis of their findings.

PIE CHART

Pie charts are helpful when considering data that presents the frequency of one numerical variable against a categorical variable. Pie charts are a representation of the proportion of responses. This might be the number or percentage of students in a study who misbehave in lessons. In one of my primary schools, a headteacher was keen to gauge the staff's perceptions of behaviour across the school. They presented the findings in a range of pie charts and used this as a pictorial representation for further analysis and discussion with staff about their perception of behaviour. Each pie chart represented the responses from different staff groups, including senior leaders, teachers, teaching assistants and pastoral staff. The pie charts allowed the headteacher to provide an overview of staff opinions by considering the overall response and comparing this to responses from the four different groups of staff across the school. As a result of this analysis, the researcher was able to pose further questions in their analysis about staff perceptions of behaviour across the school.

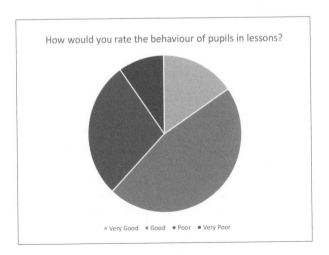

How would you rate the behaviour of pupils in lessons?

▪ Very Good ▪ Good ▪ Poor ▪ Very Poor

PERCENTAGE COMPONENT BAR CHARTS

Percentage component charts help the researcher to spot the extent of the differences between variables. Rather than producing four separate pie charts, as in the example just now, the percentage component chart can produce this data on one chart, allowing the researcher to eyeball for similarities, differences and anomalies in their data. Returning to the example where the headteacher surveyed their staff to seek their opinion on the behaviour of pupils in lessons, the researcher can now place responses from all staff, teachers, teaching assistants and senior leaders on one chart:

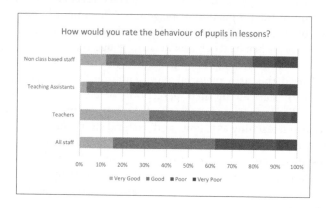

The data can now be compared across the three staff groups, allowing the researcher to pose further questions in the analysis. For example, why do a greater proportion of teaching assistants appear to think behaviour in lessons is poor when compared to teachers?

SPIDER CHART

The spider chart, also called a radar chart, is a form of line graph. It helps the researcher to represent their data in a chart that shows the relative size of a response on one scale for interrelated variables. Like the bar chart, the data needs to have one scale which is common to all variables. The spider chart is drawn with the variables spanning the chart, creating a spider web. An example of this is seen in a research study looking at self-reported confidence in year 7 students across a range of subjects taught in their first term in secondary school. The researcher takes the responses from a sample group and calculates the mean to plot on the spider chart. The spider chart allows the researcher to easily compare and contrast the confidence level in different subjects for the sample group. The chart, like the pie chart, can then be broken down for different groups of students within the study – perhaps by gender or attainment – in order to elicit further analysis of findings.

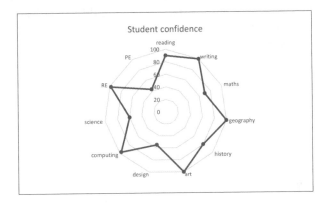

LINE CHART

A line chart is really helpful when interpreting data over time. An example of this is a researcher considering the reading age of a pupil who has been given a new intervention. The chart allows the researcher to see the progress of the pupil at regular time intervals and analyse the effect of the programme on the pupil's reading.

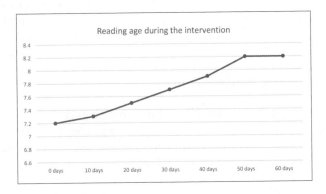

SCATTER CHART

A line chart is helpful when comparing two scaled variables. An example of two scaled variables could be a comparison of enjoyment of science for a group of year 10 low-achieving students at two different points in time. This may be at the start of introducing a new initiative and after three months of implementation. This is represented on the scatter chart below with the starting measure on the horizontal axis and the final measure on the vertical axis for a sample group of ten pupils. The line represents the status quo, where there is no change in enjoyment from the start and end of this study. Those dots that appear above the line show improved enjoyment and those below the line show diminished enjoyment.

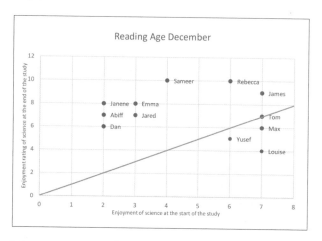

From this data, we may pose the question as to why it seems the student that showed a greater enjoyment of science at the start of the programme appears to have less enjoyment by the end of the programme, as seen with Max, Yusef and Louise. Also, the researcher may like to interrogate why those students who enjoyed science the least at the start of the programme appear to have increased their enjoyment to a similar level to other students in the group, as seen with Janene, Emma, Jared, Abiff and Dan.

Key questions when eyeballing data and charts

Eyeballing data is an art that you can get better at with practice. In order to strengthen your ability to eyeball data, you can ask the following critical questions as you examine the data and charts:

- **Stepping back** from your data, what jumps out at you?
- What are the prominent **similarities** in the data presented and why might this be the case?
- What are the prominent **differences** in the data presented and why might this be the case?

- What **didn't you expect to see** in this data?
- Does anything **support your assumptions** relating to your research question?
- Does anything **challenge your assumptions** relating to your research question?
- Is there anything in this chart that stands out as **unusual or surprising**?
- Does your **wider evidence** base **support or challenge** what you see in this data?
- Can you **trust** this data? Why?
- Are there any **other ways** you can **represent your data?** Would a different chart help you see something new?
- How does **X affect Y**?
- Is there anything that you would have **changed** in your methodology now you have analysed this data?

Conclusion of step 6

The analysis of data can involve words, images and numbers. By analysing the qualitative words and images, you learn to read data to seek for similarities, differences and anomalies. Visual maps can be useful to present your findings and highlight patterns within your data, helping you to visualise the information gathered. Synthesising and analysing the data in order to draw out relevant information will help you answer your research question.

Quantitative data can be displayed through a range of graphical representations. This can also include qualitative data that has been converted into numbers. The charts produced from the data help you to spot patterns and anomalies as you develop the skill of eyeballing the information. In eyeballing the data, using the key questions outlined in this step, you can become increasingly effective at drawing out meaning to answer your research question and inform your conclusions, helping you to move to sharing your new understanding at step 7 of the Research Cycle.

Finally, you must remain cautious when analysing your data. Be tentative in your analysis of findings and don't let the data trick you into making wild and far-reaching statements. You must recognise your own bias and be open to what your analysis suggests, even if this goes against your own assumptions or hopes for the research. With all this in mind, you are now ready to move to step 7 as you begin to think about how you can share your new understanding with others.

Key messages from step 6
'Analyse the findings'

- **Analysis** is the art of unpacking or **breaking down the data** for analysis in order to bring clarity to what the data is saying.
- **Synthesis** is the art of **drawing together the many elements** of data in order to form a conclusion.
- **Seek out data that is helpful** in answering your research question.
- When analysing words, use the **constant comparative method** to seek out patterns to compare similarities, differences and anomalies in the data.
- Help define **cause and effect** within research through the use of a **flow map**.
- **Compare and contrast** data using a **double bubble map**.
- The **tree map** helps you sort data into **categories**.
- While not essential in the analysis of data, **words and images (qualitative data)** can be turned into **numbers (quantitative data)** to broaden the analysis of the data.
- **Eyeballing** is the process of **reading and rereading data** to seek for **relevant patterns** or **anomalies** in the data set.
- **Bar charts** are helpful when comparing the **frequency** of a measurement across a range of variables.
- The **distribution chart** uses a range rather than a single number in a data set, helping to **group larger data sets into bite sized** chunks of data that is easier to interpret.
- **Pie charts** are helpful when presenting data relating to the **frequency of one numerical variable against a categorical variable**.
- **Percentage component bar** charts compare percentage responses across **multiple sets of data**.
- **A spider or radar chart** presents data visually showing the **relative scale of response** on a common scale for a range of variables.
- **Line charts** are helpful when interpreting data at a range of **points in time**.
- **Scatter charts** group data to present patterns when looking at **two scaled variables**.
- When analysing the data, you must **hold your assumptions lightly** in order to allow the data to tell the story of research.
- Be alert to your own **conscious or unconscious bias** in your analysis and when answering your research question.

THE RESEARCH CYCLE
Step 7: Share the new understanding

Now you have completed the analysis of data at step 6 of the Research Cycle, you are ready to share the key points you have discovered. It is important to be aware of step 7 in the Research Cycle at the outset of the research journey. In knowing that you will be required to present your research findings, you embark on the Research Cycle with a potential audience in mind, encouraging you to maintain the quality and integrity of your research as it unfolds. In short, by keeping the end point in mind, you recognise the importance of making your research accessible to your potential audience, whether this is your team leader, appraisal lead, colleagues, senior staff or colleagues beyond your own organisation.

There are many ways to share your research findings, such as a structured article to be published in an organisational research journal, a digital presentation or notes to support a verbal presentation to a group of colleagues. It is important that you take ownership of this step in the Research Cycle; in doing so, you will become increasingly confident about sharing your research findings with others. The thought of sharing the new understanding from your research analysis – in particular, presenting findings to a wider audience of colleagues – can often make researchers feel nervous. I find that with a gentle nudge, the researcher is encouraged to step outside their comfort zone to present their findings, helping them to grow professionally. My advice to you is to be brave and speak with your research coach about the most effective method of sharing your new understanding. If you are nervous about presenting, use your research coach to help you to gain confidence; you will be amazed at what you can achieve in this step of the Research Cycle by sharing your findings with others within your organisation and beyond.

Let us now consider a range of strategies to help you to share your research findings. My advice is to find a strategy that appeals to you or one that fits well with the research findings you have to share.

Journal write-up

In my trust, we publish a research journal called *Irresistible Learning*. The journal is a real inspiration, sharing the research outcomes from our staff across the trust. Articles are included from both the curriculum and business staff teams. In order for researchers to present their findings, I provide a structure to the articles. Each article follows this format:

Research question – the refined research question from step 4 of the Research Cycle is shared to act as a clear reference point to the article.

Rationale – the researcher outlines the reason why they have chosen this field of study. This may include elements of step 3 of the Research Cycle as they draw on what is already known about their field of study and what guided their research question, including the relevance to them or their organisation.

Methodology – here the researcher explains the research methods chosen from step 5 of the Research Cycle.

Main findings – key messages and findings from the analysis and synthesis of data in step 6 are shared in this section. This should tell a story and help the reader to see what the researcher has found in their analysis of data.

Conclusion – the researcher then makes a final concluding statement about their research. The researcher should also, where possible, share their thoughts on how their conclusion will impact on future practice, echoing steps 6–8 of the Research Cycle.

Following this structure, the researcher remains focused on sharing their research findings in a succinct and precise manner. The journal articles are not highly referenced academic pieces; they are not peer-reviewed by professors. However, the articles are deeply relevant to the daily practice within the organisation and have been quality-assured by the research leads within the organisation. I edit each article to ensure the content is clear before publication and always swell with a sense of pride in my staff team as I undertake this task.

Blog

Like the journal write-up, producing a blog encourages you to think carefully about how you can present your research findings to an audience. While the blog can follow a similar format to the journal article, it also allows the writer to include hyperlinks to other research, articles or points of interest online. As an example, a researcher writing about memory techniques can link to a video of Tony Buzan explaining mind-mapping, an online journal article they have used and a helpful book for further reading available from a digital bookshop.

Blog articles can also be shared easily with colleagues within and beyond your organisation. Using social media as a platform to share the blog grows your potential audience exponentially. Blogs that have been written by staff can also be published on the school or trust website, building professional kudos for research both within and beyond the organisation.

Here are my top tips for using a blog to share your new understanding:

- Follow the **format for the journal** write-up to help structure your blog.
- Write your blog as a **narrative** to tell the story of your research findings.
- Use **hyperlinks** to relevant books, journals, videos and websites to build connections and interest to the reader.
- Link your blog to **social media networks** such as Twitter, Facebook, LinkedIn or Instagram.
- **Follow others** in your professional network to build interest in your blog and encourage debate.
- **Share** your blog widely.
- Link your blog (with permission) to your **organisation's website**.
- Be prepared to **receive critique** from others who may challenge your findings.

Digital presentation

Building a digital presentation in a program such as Microsoft PowerPoint can be a really helpful way to crystallise how to present your findings. The format of the digital presentation encourages you to use fewer words, coupled with graphical representation or pictures, to tell the story of your research findings. As a researcher, you can write a narrative or further bullet points in the notes section to help you keep on track with what needs to be said when delivering the presentation.

You can use digital presentation tools, like Microsoft PowerPoint, to record a narrated commentary to your presentation. This is really useful when sharing new understanding from research with a wide audience. Narrated presentations are also helpful if you are nervous about presenting live, as you can rehearse and record the narrative for each slide using audio or a video. Once created, the narrated presentation can be exported as a video and shared widely through social media on platforms such as YouTube.

I have used prezi.com as a digital presentation tool. Prezi, available free of charge to those working in education, is a three-dimensional presentation platform that can zoom in and out on a virtual three-dimensional piece of paper. Prezi, like Microsoft Powerpoint, uses words and images to present findings.

There are also a range of animation platforms available. Tools like Doodly allow you to use images and cartoons to create a narrated presentation that is both engaging and fun to share. These presentation tools use a mixture of drawn images and words during the presentation, coupled with a narration and even a backing soundtrack. If you are nervous speaking to a live audience, or want to produce a video explaining your research outcomes to a wider audience on social media, get creative and explore these or other platforms available to you.

Video recording

As with the narrated presentations using Microsoft PowerPoint, a video recording can provide the researcher who is anxious about presentation with a less threatening means of sharing their research findings with a wider audience. You don't need to depend on specialist recording equipment; you can just use a phone to record your voice or image and then share it with a wider audience. One of my staff undertook a research project into the development of a sensory room and used a school tablet device to record their research journey. The video also included children using the sensory room. Their inclusion brought the presentation to life as the researcher was able to demonstrate how the research had led to the creation of a meaningful space for our sensory challenged pupils.

There are a range of audio and visual applications available to support the recording of presentations. From the simplest voice recording applications found on a smartphone to more complex applications, you can use these to record sound and video to present your new understanding.

When recording, you need to be mindful of the ethics of using the images of other adults and students. Full permissions must be sought and the organisation's data protection manager needs to be informed of the platforms you use to record the images or voice, as these are classed as personal data.

Small group presentation

While some researchers may be worried about presenting to a wide audience, they may feel more comfortable presenting their research study to a smaller group of their peers within their team. Our teaching assistants can often feel a little anxious when presenting to teachers and senior leaders. In these circumstances, the research coach will give researchers the opportunity to present their findings to a smaller group of peers. This allows the researcher to share their findings with colleagues who are likely to benefit the most. In order to gain the most from the presentation, participants are also briefed to ask questions about the presentations as this often elicits a deeper understanding of the research for both the participants and the researcher.

Research poster

A research poster is a simple yet engaging way to present research findings in a format that is easy to digest. Using the format of the journal article, the poster allows the researcher to present their findings in a way that can be browsed by colleagues. The poster can also be a reference tool for the researcher to use during a presentation to a small group of colleagues. I have used research posters as a marketplace of ideas during a presentation of research. In the marketplace, the research posters are mounted on easels around the room so that staff can wander amongst them and discuss their content.

I ran a research project with a group of middle leaders across ten primary schools. The final stage of the project was to share the research findings and the researchers gave a two-minute presentation to the delegates from their schools. This was followed with a marketplace of the ten research projects where the research posters were used as a talking point for each researcher as delegates wandered freely around the hall. The casual atmosphere of the marketplace allowed staff to pose questions to the researchers about their research posters and gain a deeper perspective about the research undertaken.

Here are some tips for creating an effective research poster, adapted from NYU Libraries (2020):

- Think about your **audience** and design your poster with them in mind.
- Make your font size **readable** from a comfortable distance away from your poster.
- Grab your readers with a **clear title/research question**.
- **Limit your words** to keep your reader engaged and to be precise in what you are communicating.

- Use **bullets, numbering, and headlines** to make it easy to read.
- Think about your **graphics and colours to enhance your poster** rather than distract the reader.
- Include **logos** from your organisation.
- Remember to put **your name** on the piece.
- Include **references** used in step 3 of the Research Cycle.
- **Share** your poster with a colleague/coach to make sure it is easy to interpret.

Here is an example of a research poster produced by two teaching assistants whose research question was, 'Can a nurture approach support pupils with complex needs to improve their behaviours?':

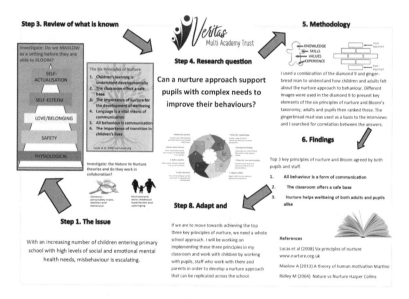

While this poster does not share the detail of the research undertaken, it allowed the researchers to share the key steps in the Research Cycle. In displaying this in a research poster, the researchers were able to talk through each step with colleagues. While this poster is not a perfect example of a research poster, I have included it to give you an idea of the form a research poster could take. My advice is to be playful and use the Research Cycle to help structure your poster.

Staff often enjoy creating research posters as it allows for creative flair. The posters can be produced digitally using programs such as Microsoft Publisher or PowerPoint or by a simple cut-and-paste onto A1 card backing.

Conclusion of step 7

Now you have drawn your conclusions and considered the next steps suggested by your research, the presentation of findings is a vital step in the Research Cycle. As a researcher, there are several ways of presenting your findings, some of which may gently push you out of your professional comfort zone. You need to think carefully about your audience when sharing new understanding about your research question. If you do not present your findings convincingly, the key messages from your research could be lost in translation. Whether you are showing your findings in a journal write-up or a verbal presentation to a small team of colleagues, step 7 in the Research Cycle gives you a chance to shine, to articulate your new learning and to impact on the pedagogy and practice of your colleagues.

Key messages from step 7
'Share the new understanding'

- Think about **sharing new understanding at step 7** at the outset of your Research Cycle, so you can keep this in mind when developing your research.
- Produce a **journal write-up** for your research and encourage your organisation to produce its own **research journal**.
- Use a **blog** as a vehicle to present your research findings and share new understanding.
- Use **digital presentation tools** such as Microsoft PowerPoint and Prezi to share your research. If you are less confident in presenting live, then record a **narrated presentation**.
- **Record your voice or a video** to present your research findings to a wider audience.
- Present to a **small group of colleagues** if you are nervous presenting to larger groups in order to show what you've discovered and build your confidence in presenting.
- A **research poster** can be a fun and engaging way to connect research findings with an audience.

THE RESEARCH CYCLE
Step 8: Adapt or affirm practice in light of what you have learnt

Research in schools empowers you to develop practice that can impact positively on your organisation. Whether you are part of the curriculum team working directly with students or the business teams working across a school or trust, research is affirming and can exemplify the effectiveness of new practice. Research can challenge existing practice and move the researcher to confront their own thinking and values. And it can also seek out fresh ideas to adapt current practice. Whatever the outcome, through research, you are led to carefully consider your next steps in adapting or affirming your own practice or influencing the wider practice of your teams.

As the educational landscape continues to shift beneath our feet, we are moving into what is a golden age for education. An age where we have seen global movement towards a decentralisation of schools, where governments have reduced the central control of schools and have devolved to a self-improving system where school leaders support colleagues to make improvements based on local context. This devolution of centralised power has created a void in which research can help to inform practice and develop pedagogy in schools.

There is also a growing interest in research-informed practice. While academic research has influenced practice and policy in schools for many years, there is a renewed passion for school-based research to help schools strengthen practice at a local level. Academic research remains important in order to guide policy and practice at a national level; however, school-based research has the ability to forge a positive and lasting impact on practice that is highly relevant to the individual school. Research in school empowers staff to become increasingly knowledgeable about their role and aware of the research of others and to be more reflective as practitioners.

The final step in the Research Cycle is to encourage you to think about the implications of your research on your own or other's practice and whether there are wider implications for the practice of the organisation. At this point in the Research Cycle, you simply need to ask yourself 'So, what…?'

So, what…

- did you **find out** relating to your research question?
- did you **not find out** that you hoped to discover?
- **surprises did you discover** along the way?
- did you find that **challenged or changed** your own practice?
- has changed in the **progress of your students** as a result of your research?
- has changed in the **relationships you have with your colleagues** as a result of your research?
- are the **implications of your research** for your team, school, organisation, network beyond the school?
- **has changed in you** as a person as a result of this research project?
- were the **pitfalls in your research** project that you will use to inform your next research cycle?
- will be your **next research question**, knowing what you now know?

This will lead to the key question relating to step 8 of the Research Cycle:

- So, what will you **do differently** as a result of your research?

As a researcher, you now need to define how you will adapt or affirm your practice in light of your research findings. This may be a personal adjustment or one that requires organisational change. Libby Nicholas and John West-Burnham (2018) talk of three tiers of organisational change: shallow, deep and profound change.

The first is **shallow change**, which they describe as tidying the garden. You may have discovered that, through your research, your practice simply needs small adjustments to make positive gains.

Deep change happens when there is a significant shift in practice. You may have found that your current practice requires a re-think. In such cases, you will need to think carefully about whether this practice will impact on others across the organisation or whether you will need approval of your senior leaders in order to effect an organisational change as a result of your research.

Finally, Nicholas and West-Burnham talk of **profound change**, or 'second curve thinking'. Profound change requires a radical and new way of operating. They equate this to the caterpillar metamorphosing into a butterfly. While it is less likely that you will be led to profound change through your research, it is possible, and both you and your organisation need to be open to the possibility that engaging in research-informed practice can lead to the status quo being challenged.

Step 8 is deeply rewarding in an organisation in which there is a culture where research outcomes are celebrated and staff have ownership of organisational change. While change for the sake of change can be unsettling to an organisation, research-informed change is often more measured and timely, leading to greater and lasting impact for the organisation.

In order to adapt future practice, you need to build an action plan. This plan could form part of the existing action planning structure within the school. Alternatively, you could use your own action planning tool. Here is an example of an action plan tool used by a teacher who is looking to develop practice in memory retention in their class as a result of a small-scale research project with a group of students:

Research question	Can the use of memory retention games help history students in year 11 to improve test outcomes?
Research findings	Retrieval practice helped students to recall 15% more key historical facts than a control group.
Proposed action	Introduce retrieval practice games into history lessons in year 11.
Key performance indicators	Teachers trained in retrieval practice theory and games. Teachers review knowledge retention of key historical facts. Pupils' test scores tracked across year 11 demonstrate 15% rise in mean performance for students.

Key milestones		
By end of December	By end of March	By end of July
Discuss the action plan with the senior team to ensure this supports school policy. Train teachers in the theory of retrieval practice. Teachers trial three retrieval activities. Meet with teachers to review best practice and discuss pitfalls.	Student test scores demonstrate 5% rise in scores. Teachers develop the use of a further three retrieval practice activities.	Student test scores demonstrate 15% rise in scores. Teachers review the impact of the retrieval practice and share the outcomes with wider departmental leads.
Impact: linked to key performance indicators	All teachers in the history department have been trained in retrieval practice theory and games and now incorporate these consistently within their planning. Students report that they enjoy the low-impact quizzing in history and that it has also improved their confidence when faced by a formal test. Scores in GCSE history rose by 14% after the first year.	

The final step of the Research Cycle encourages you to move on to step 1 of your next Research Cycle. Research is a flow of activity. It may be that you have unpacked a range of further questions about your own practice that naturally lead to the formulation of a new issue to research. This may not be the case and the next phase of research may take you to a completely new issue. In either case, you will have learnt more about yourself, your organisation, your colleagues and your students. You will bring your new learning to bear when engaging in the next Research Cycle and continue to strengthen your practice, your confidence and your capacity for research, strengthening your organisation in the process, leading to a richer offer for the students and a truly irresistible school where all members of the school community are excited about research.

Lethal mutations

While research has great potential in defining new practice that is highly effective in supporting learning, there is a danger that when research outcomes are shared across the organisation, the context and detail of what makes the practice successful can be lost. This is particularly risky when sharing practice that research suggests is highly effective in a particular context. Dylan Wiliam (2018) talks of the concept of lethal mutation first developed by Edward Haertel. A lethal mutation occurs when research findings are used to inform new practice but the practice underpinning the research is not adhered to or fully understood, thus changing or mutating the practice. By oversimplifying the research outcome, the user then misrepresents the practice, leading to the lethal mutation that often diminishes the effectiveness of the practice outlined in the research.

It is important that, as a researcher, you recognise the risk of lethal mutation. When planning your own research question, be aware that, as you work through step 3 of the Research Cycle and find out what is already known, you are mindful of lethal mutations in the research of others. You also need to be cognisant of the risk in assuming practice shared by others will be mirrored in your own context and that you are not inadvertently forming a lethal mutation from the research findings of others. Equally, when sharing your own research findings at step 7 or adapting practice at step 8 of the Research Cycle, you must be cautious to emphasise the context in which your research operated and share, with clarity, the potential limitations or difficulties in replicating the new practice elsewhere.

Lethal mutations are often inevitable when sharing research findings. As a researcher, you need to be alert to how easily your research or the research and practice of others can mutate when engaging in research practice. It is worth noting that not all mutations have a negative effect on outcomes in practice –

they can sometimes be positive. While lethal mutations are inevitable, you need to call them out when you see them, in particular when planning your own research, or sharing your research outcomes with others.

Conclusion of step 8

Once you have shared your research findings across the organisation, you need to consider how to adapt and affirm your practice in light of what you have learnt. This step in the Research Cycle will ask you to think about, adjust or refine your own practice or the practice of others. It can be challenging if your research findings suggest that you do need to make amendments within your organisation. It is important to think carefully about how to implement the changes suggested by your research and, in this process, to bring colleagues along with you to ensure change is manageable, purposeful and lasting. Action planning can help this process as it allows you to share your intentions with your colleagues. You also need to be alert to lethal mutations that can arise from the research of others and your own research findings, guiding colleagues in the new practice suggested by your research findings, so practice is not misinterpreted and the impact lost.

Finally, as you reach the conclusion of the Research Cycle, it is time to think forward to your next Research Cycle. There may have been elements of your research that sparked further research questions. You may also have listened with interest to colleagues whose presentations of research findings resonated with you. The Research Cycle has a flow, and once embedded in your organisation, it becomes a helpful tool to support the structure of your research practice and the practice of your colleagues.

Key messages from step 8
'Adapt or affirm practice in light of what you have learnt'

- Ask **'So, what...?' questions** to help affirm the impact of your research study.
- Consider whether your research leads to **shallow, deep or profound change**.
- Think about **who else needs to be involved** in adapting or affirming practice.
- Use an **action plan** to structure the next steps leading from the research findings.
- When sharing research, consider the impact of **lethal mutations** as this can adversely affect the replication of practice from your research findings.
- Think about any elements of your research or the research of others that **fuelled interest or resonated** with you as you start to think about the next cycle of research.

Key messages from chapter 2 'Research Methodology'

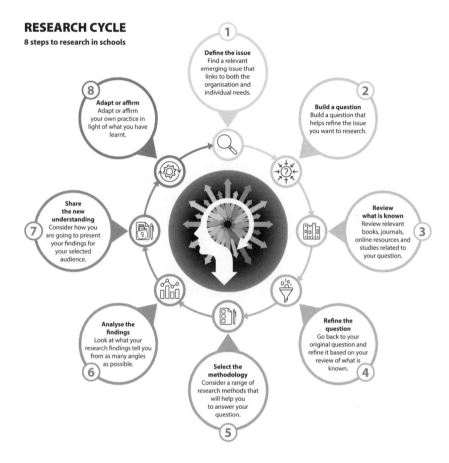

RESEARCH CYCLE
8 steps to research in schools

1 Define the issue
Find a relevant emerging issue that links to both the organisation and individual needs.

2 Build a question
Build a question that helps refine the issue you want to research.

3 Review what is known
Review relevant books, journals, online resources and studies related to your question.

4 Refine the question
Go back to your original question and refine it based on your review of what is known.

5 Select the methodology
Consider a range of research methods that will help you to answer your question.

6 Analyse the findings
Look at what your research findings tell you from as many angles as possible.

7 Share the new understanding
Consider how you are going to present your findings for your selected audience.

8 Adapt or affirm
Adapt or affirm your own practice in light of what you have learnt.

- **Step 1 – 'Define the issue'** – find an issue worthy of research that is purposeful to both you and your organisation.
- **Step 2 – 'Build a question to answer the issue'** – craft a question that helps you refine your field of study.
- **Step 3 – 'Review what is known about the issue'** – review literature and websites and engage in meaningful discussions to broaden your understanding of your field of study. Try to understand the vulnerabilities in what you discover and grapple with your own bias and the bias of others.

- **Step 4 – 'Refine the question'** – return to your original research question to ensure it is still the right question. If not, refine the question.
- **Step 5 – 'Select the research methodology'** – understand the theory behind research methodology and be playful with the research methodologies available to you. Select the best research tools to answer your research question.
- **Step 6 – 'Analyse the findings'** – cast a knowledgeable eye over your research findings. Whether the findings are numbers, words or pictures, use this to seek patterns that help you draw meaningful conclusions from your research.
- **Step 7 – 'Share the new understanding'** – think about how to share your findings. Be brave in this step. Think about this early in the research process to keep your potential audience in mind.
- **Step 8 – 'Adapt or affirm practice in light of what you have learnt'** – remember that research in schools is about either affirming practice or adapting practice; ensure the fruits of your research help strengthen your own and others' practice.

Chapter 3
Creating a culture of research

Having explained how you can use the Research Cycle as a tool to strengthen your research practice, it is now time to share a range of strategies that can be used by school leaders to introduce and embed research practice across the organisation. By school leaders, I am not referring exclusively to the headteacher, but rather any member of the school team with a leadership role. School leaders can include headteachers, deputy headteachers, governors, subject leaders, phase leaders and leaders from within the curriculum or business teams. As you read on, consider the strategies I outline through the leadership lens relevant to your roles and responsibilities.

While creating a lasting culture of research in school is a complex task amidst the myriad of demands faced by school leaders; it remains a worthy challenge. Embedding a culture of research provides valuable rewards for the school, its staff and its pupils. Research in school helps to build a culture that fuels optimism, professionalism and possibility and creates a palpable feeling of excitement. John West-Burnham (2009) puts this simply:

> There is no doubt that transformation can be emotionally exhilarating and intellectually exciting but at the same time there has to be a deep and rigorous justification to avoid the accusation of 'change for change's sake' and to secure commitment through consensus and engagement rather than control and compliance.

The power of research to be emotionally exhilarating and intellectually exciting to both school leaders and staff alike provides a catalyst to organisational change. As West-Burnham suggests in the quote above, research encourages deep ownership of the strategic journey of the school as each member of staff plays their part in informing the direction of travel through their research activity.

Building a culture of research in schools takes time and vision. The culture starts with a range of systems that support research, supported by the methodologies within each step of the Research Cycle. While the process of building the culture of research in schools can be complex, it is often a greater challenge to maintain the culture and ensure research practice is embedded across the organisation. I will now explore a range of systems that I have used to embed a culture of research practice in my schools that leads to a climate where relationships grow and professionalism strengthens.

Culture and climate

Now I have explained the practical theory and practice of research through the eight steps of the Research Cycle, I will now go on to explore how to create a culture of research with a climate where research can flourish. Creating a culture of research in school has a deep and lasting impact on the engagement of staff through their ownership of the organisation's strategic journey. Creating a culture and climate where research practice can flourish is essential to ensure research practice is embedded and supports the growth of staff and positive outcomes for students.

Let me start by defining what I mean by culture and climate. Put simply, culture is the organisational structure put in place in schools and the climate is the feeling this culture creates. The culture includes the school's leadership structure, policies and practice, the unwritten traditions and rituals built up over time. The climate is influenced by the relationships between staff, how safe staff feel, the physical environment, the joy of teaching, the love of their role, feeling valued, a feeling of love for the school. Climate is the heart and soul of the school. This chapter will explore strategies that help build a culture and climate for research in school. These methods are tried and tested within my schools and have led to the strengthening of research practice in staff.

In building a strong culture of research in school, the school leader needs to put in place a range of systems that create space and purpose for research-engaged staff. In busy schools, it is all too easy to introduce a system for research and enjoy a short-term impact. If you are to enact a cultural change, the systems need to be embedded in the long-term habitual practice of your school. This takes tenacity and diligence from school leaders to make sure that the system is introduced to staff, the value of each system is maintained and revisited regularly, and new staff are carefully inducted into the systems. This helps research to become tacit: like riding a bike or standing on one leg, you can simply do it without conscious thought because it is just the way things are done.

In building a culture of research – or indeed any one of the systems I will outline in this book – you need to begin with ensuring your staff are with you. Building a culture of 'followship' is pivotal to creating a climate where staff feel inspired by research practice. Blakesley (2012) defines 'followship' as a leadership strategy that encourages 'superb performers to follow passionate leaders'. Blakesley explores six steps in followship:

1. KNOW THYSELF

In building a culture of research in school, the leader needs to be clear about their own motivations. In knowing thyself, the school leader is asked to see themselves through others' eyes. A leader that understands their staff's perspective will be better poised to see the advantages and potential pitfalls in introducing systems of research practice. The leader will understand the different perspectives of staff who have been through university-based research and those who have never been asked to engage in research. In knowing themselves, the school leader begins to understand their staff. Equally, if the school leader has gaps in their own strengths, they can build and utilise their team to make up for them.

2. HAVE THE RIGHT PERSPECTIVE

When thinking about the right perspective, the school leader needs to be clear about how they fit into the organisation. This is also important for school staff. If staff do not see where they fit in the school, they struggle with the role they can play. This is true also of the relevance of research in schools. When encouraging a member of staff to engage in research practice, they need to have clarity in their own roles and responsibilities as well as how these fit into the key priorities for the school or trust in which they belong. They need to see relevance and purpose to their research, for both themselves, their students and their organisation.

The school leader also needs to understand the importance of using the strengths within their staff. Later in this book, I will consider talent pathways – a way for a leader to spot talent in their staff and encourage research that strengthens the career pathway of their staff. A recognition that staff will hold different strengths and talents is important. Blakesley puts it eloquently (2012): 'Don't waste time trying to put into someone something that isn't there, because it is hard enough to get out what is already there.' The school leader therefore needs to be astute in knowing their staff and guiding their research practice to ensure it has meaning for the researcher and the organisation. The leader also needs to help the researcher to grow in their own career pathway.

3. SEE WHAT IS UNDER THE HOOD

Blakesley uses the analogy of cars in a showroom. Two seemingly identical cars can perform very differently as they have different engines under the bonnet (or hood). This step in encouraging followship asks the school leader to know their staff's talents and what makes them tick, understanding beyond what and how your staff think and considering what and how your staff feel. Blakesley puts it succinctly in the phrase 'Get to know your people in ways they don't expect.' A third dimension to knowing your staff is to understand them on a spiritual level. This is not a religious dimension but rather involves an understanding of the core purpose and motivations held by staff, the values that are deeply set in each individual. Understanding the intelligence, emotional and spiritual drivers in your staff can help build strong relationships in the workplace. The impact on research practice is also amplified through knowing what is under the bonnet. The clarity of understanding can help you to support your researcher in their research practice as you guide them to meaningful research that truly resonates with them at the core of where their intelligence, emotions and spiritual self coincide.

4. BUILD TRUST

The importance of mutual trust between a leader and their employees has been well documented in texts relating to organisational management. In building a culture of trust, Blakesley outlines five helpful qualities of a leader who is encouraging a culture of followship:

Integrity – ensure you stick to your promises as this helps build trust and relationships with your employees.

Listening – a firm belief that 'none of us are as smart as all of us'. The acknowledgement that a leader cannot come up with all the ideas in isolation but that the organisation grows through the innovation of its employees is pivotal to empowering the culture of research in schools. Leaders at every level need to be encouraged to listen to their staff, and research practice provides a powerful route to formalise this process of active listening.

Accountability – a leader must be willing to take the blame when things do not go to plan. In the frame of building a culture of research in school, the school leaders need to accept that in using research to trial new practice, there will be times when things go wrong or do not go to plan. At these points, it is important that employees see the school leaders being honest about what is not working and accepting when their employees' research does not provide the impact hoped for. Building a culture where staff can throw their hands in the air when this happens and learn from their research is pivotal.

Respect – school leaders must build a genuine respect for others. This is all the more difficult when trust has been broken. The school leader must show their integrity, listen to their staff and demonstrate their humility when things go wrong in order to build respect in their staff. Research practice can provide a genuine means of building respect as a well-constructed research project demonstrates the integrity and value of a member of the staff team.

Loyalty – this final quality in building trust requires school leaders to be actively involved in achieving the goals set. The leaders need to be genuinely interested in the research practice of their staff. Opportunities for staff to share their research outcomes with their school leaders is important as this will build trust and loyalty in the staff team.

5. GOAL SETTING

Goals provide the vision of the leader. They help the employees get their teeth into the purpose of their work. In research-active schools, the goals of the organisation act as a beacon to race towards. Each researcher needs to understand the key priorities for the school and/or trust in which they work. This gives a focus to the research work in the school and helps staff to align their research practice, so that everyone in the organisation is moving in a similar direction with their research.

6. BE EMOTIONALLY COMPETENT

While we have looked at emotional intelligence and what is under the bonnet, the school leader needs to be aware of the emotions of staff and the source of these emotions. Blakesley puts it like this: 'Emotions are chemical reactions that cause physiological changes in the body to produce protective behaviours.' As a leader, you need to consider the emotions in your staff when engaging in research practice as these can be powerful motivators to helping your researcher to truly own their research project. It may also be your role to help your researcher recognise these emotions in themselves and others and manage these feelings through spotting the triggers and identifying troublesome emotions.

The concept of followship is helpful in building a positive culture and climate of research in schools. In strengthening the desire to move together as researchers, a staff team can achieve more than the sum of its parts. In building the systems, the school culture is strengthened, and through followship, the climate of the school is enhanced. A research-engaged school therefore provides the platform to develop the emotional heart of the school.

Appraisal

Appraisal provides a helpful framework for embedding a culture of research in schools. The appraisal cycle gives the researcher a clear timeframe and scaffold upon which their research can take place. Using the research cycle, the appraiser can act as research coach, building a symbiotic relationship between research and appraisal across the organisation.

In our schools, each member of staff has at least one research-based appraisal target. The target follows three guiding principles and is formally discussed at three points in the appraisal cycle:

1. INITIAL APPRAISAL MEETING – DEVISE A MEANINGFUL RESEARCH QUESTION (STEPS 1–4 IN THE RESEARCH CYCLE)

The researcher will be guided to think about their current job roles and responsibilities. Through a coaching discussion, the researcher is asked to reflect on their current strengths and challenges. These are brought alongside the organisation's own priorities to find where there may be connections. The researcher is then asked to pinpoint general areas that could form into a purposeful research question. This is step 1 of the Research Cycle as the researcher is asked to define the issue. At this point, the appraisal cycle and the Research Cycle for this target become one and the employee is now being coached in research practice by their appraiser.

Building on the Research Cycle at step 2, the appraiser then helps the researcher construct their research question. This helps the researcher build the link between their research interests and the organisational priorities. It is also a great opportunity to find that sweet spot between your researcher's intelligence, emotion and spirit that gives their research depth of relevance, meaning and purpose. The connection between personal relevance and organisational relevance helps build the culture of followship as the individual aligns their research to that being undertaken by colleagues in the school.. The appraiser will then take the researcher through the Research Cycle to support them in the journey of bringing their research project to fruition.

2. MID-YEAR APPRAISAL REVIEW – ENGAGE IN A RESEARCH (STEPS 5–6 IN THE RESEARCH CYCLE)

The appraiser, as research coach, will then guide their researcher through the research methodologies needed to investigate their research question at step 5 of the Research Cycle. This process supports the appraisee to strengthen their research practice and move purposefully toward the analysis of data at step 6 of the Research Cycle. The research practice at step 5 often falls around the point of mid-year review. This allows the appraiser to support the researcher in their research activity, to ensure the Research Cycle remains on track. This helps to keep the flow of research moving forward in the school and maintains the pace in the Research Cycle for all staff.

If your researcher has undertaken their research activity, they may be grappling with the analysis of data. The mid-year review then becomes a useful point for the appraiser, as research coach, to help the researcher to think through their data analysis and help them to crystallise their analysis using a range of relevant graphical or visual representations.

3. FINAL APPRAISAL REVIEW – SHARE THE FINDINGS (STEPS 7–8 IN THE RESEARCH CYCLE)

It is vital that our researcher understands the importance of sharing their findings. This helps the researcher focus on the end point of their research and build their evidence with an audience in mind. The understanding that research undertaken will support the school to strengthen its practice is a powerful tool for building purpose in the research. Discussing step 7 of the Research Cycle at the outset of the appraisal cycle allows the appraiser to coach the researcher in building their confidence to present. This is often a bold step for staff who are not used to presenting to others.

The appraisal cycle builds in formal review points through the year and keeps the conversations about research live between appraiser and employee. We use a digital appraisal system to record progress towards research targets. This allows the researcher to upload a narrative of their research as it unfolds. Recording progress towards their research targets helps the researcher to maintain a constant conversation between researcher and appraiser. Researchers are asked to be evaluative in their comments, to think about how their research is impacting on their practice, the practice of others, the performance of students and impact beyond their organisation. This provides a rich evidence trail for the appraisal review.

The final appraisal review reflects on the research outcomes. As this is linked to the appraisal process, no research question in the school is overlooked. Staff know their research will be reviewed and feel a sense of pride in this as they know their work will be quality-assured by their appraiser. At the point of appraisal review, the appraisers ascertain how the research will be shared. We use a range of systems in school, including the production of our own research journal, presentations to staff groups, presentations at TeachMeets, recorded commentaries and posters. By including research into the cycle of appraisal, we ensure a culture of research is embedded for all staff across the school.

In building a culture of research, the school leader can fit the Research Cycle into existing systems and structures, including the school improvement cycle and appraisal cycle, providing a purposeful platform where research practice can grow.

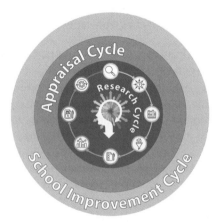

Talent pathways

I have introduced a system of talent pathways across my schools. Talent pathways are professional development pathways for staff at every level across the organisation. They map out professional development opportunities for staff that lead to strengthening practice and opportunities for career progression (Chisnell, 2021). The pathways available to our staff and volunteers are outlined in the graphic below:

I first came across the concept of talent pathways in the sporting fraternity. At a local club level, a budding rugby player will be nurtured by their club coach. As they begin to shine, the coach provides opportunities for the player to develop their skills in a number of positions. This may lead to captaincy of the team. The building of confidence and skills then lead to the county team coach noticing the player, visiting the club and watching them play. This talent-management process then continues at county level, and so on. I then considered if this system works in spotting talent in rugby: are these principles transferrable schools? Moreover, can these principles be applied to all staff rather than spotting just those with exceptional talent?

During my research trip to Singapore on behalf of the British Council, I spent a week working alongside Singaporean educators. I became particularly interested in the system the Singaporean Ministry of Education had for developing their teachers (Chisnell, 2021). When a teacher enters their first appointment in a Singaporean school, their headteacher begins a journey where they consider the teacher's future pathway. The headteacher makes a decision as to whether the teacher enters one of three pathways to a future career:

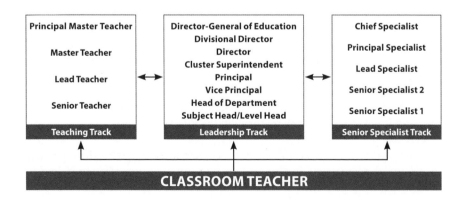

The Singaporean Ministry of Education actively seeks to identify and select future school leaders that will embody the values of the ministry. School principals support this process by completing a 'current estimated potential' form that indicates the key area of potential for each of their teachers based on appraisal outcomes which ultimately results in a ranked list. The principal will indicate in which area the teacher has particular strengths linked to the three career tracks within the system – teaching, leadership or specialist. Cluster superintendents, who are in charge of a group of 10–12 schools, meet with the school principal to review the ranked list of teachers. The cluster superintendent will then take forward the names of teachers who have significant potential in any of the three areas to the ministry, who will subsequently work with the cluster superintendent and school principal to develop opportunities to extend the teacher's skill set while testing their capacity for future leadership or specialism.

The Singapore Ministry of Education uses the ARC model of support, namely providing opportunities for teachers to undertake Assignments, develop their Relationships as a leader and attend relevant Courses. Assignments can include leading a project in school or for the Ministry of Education. Relationships are developed through opportunities to lead and develop groups of people. Courses are provided to deepen the teachers' understanding of leadership theory, subject content and successful practice. This ARC approach provides a wealth of opportunities for the teacher while informing the cluster superintendent of the teacher's potential as a school leader or specialist.

With the concept of talent management in mind, the research coach can take this idea and use it to target and nurture future research champions in the school. This is a concept that I have introduced in my trust, and we have a training programme in place for staff who show a flair or demonstrate an interest in research practice. Building on the ARC approach, staff are placed on the research talent pathway and given research-based assignments to develop their practice and confidence in leading research within teams across the trust. Assignments include the delivery of research methodology training to a team of staff. Relationships are built between the research coach and their team through the process. We also offer courses to build the skill set of our research champions. These include research coach training courses to develop the capacity to coach researchers through the Research Cycle.

The Singaporean approach to career development left me with the challenge of placing the best parts of this system into my own organisation. I had to recognise the political and cultural differences between our two jurisdictions. I also had to ensure that the talent pathway approach matched the context of not just teachers but all staff working in my schools and trust. I will now explore the key elements of our talent pathways and how they support the culture and climate of research across schools.

VOLUNTEER PATHWAY

In creating the volunteer pathway, I wanted to give a clear message to every adult offering their time in school that there was a pathway for them. The volunteer pathway is open to our volunteers and provides a range of opportunities for career development and research practice. We offer accredited training to become teaching assistants and have a trained member of staff who supports the local college in NVQ assessments. Our volunteers are often parents who have more time on their hands as their children are enrolled in school. We help our volunteers find a future pathway, and those who are interested in finding out more about life in school are supported by a mentor. While our volunteer pathway does not explicitly involve our volunteers in research, it builds a pathway towards research as they work alongside staff undertaking research projects across the schools. Research outcomes are shared with our volunteers who receive a copy of our research journal, building a connection with research at an early stage in the volunteer's journey within the school.

TEACHING ASSISTANT PATHWAY

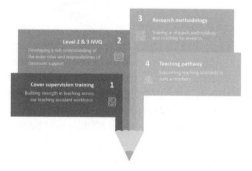

We are committed to building a highly professional team of teaching assistants across our schools. Our teaching assistant talent pathway offers a bespoke training programme to deepen the skills and professional status of our teaching assistants. Our cover supervisor course is offered to teaching assistants who want to develop their skills in teaching. This course develops a deep awareness of skills, knowledge and understanding about teaching and builds confidence in our teaching assistants in cover supervision and enhances their capacity to support learning in class. More formal training is offered on the teaching assistant pathway through level 2 and level 3 NVQ and for those who aspire for more through the higher level teaching assistant accreditation. Teaching assistants are also supported through training by our trust research and development lead. This includes bespoke training on research methodology as part of the Research Cycle, support for research writing and coaching throughout the Research Cycle. Our teaching assistant pathway helps to build a team of highly skilled teaching assistants across our schools, developing a bedrock of practice and knowledge that underpins the research questions undertaken by the teaching assistants. Teaching assistants who relish their role in teaching are also supported through the steps to become a qualified teacher and moved through to the teaching pathway, growing teachers from within the network of schools.

TEACHING PATHWAY

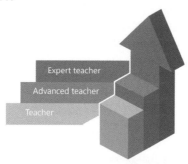

There are a range of opportunities for our teachers in the teacher pathway. These include support for staff who want to train to become a qualified teacher through diploma-, degree- or school-based training routes. For qualified teachers, the advanced teacher pathway provides opportunities for our teachers to develop their craft. Opportunities include support on national programmes such as the National Professional Qualification for Middle and Senior Leadership. Our teachers receive a bursary to enrol as a member of the Chartered College of Teaching to support their research-informed learning.

Opportunities to lead are developed through sponsorship for applications to become a chartered teacher, through postgraduate degrees and through our established culture of coaching. Our pay structure for teachers within the trust follows a three-stage development. The teacher phase ensures our early-career teachers receive the nurturement they need to embed their skills as a teacher through mentoring from an established teacher.

The teaching pathway takes the teacher from their early career development through to becoming an expert teacher. The talent pathway model is not linear, as a teacher's future pathway is not a fixed route, but rather an aspirational path for all. Teachers are supported through coaching in their first three years in the school. Early-career teachers are put into a professional learning community or linked to a research buddy who is pursuing a similar research question, where they develop research skills and self-reflective practice. As teachers develop their skills, they are given subject leadership responsibilities, and through our subject hub system, where subjects are clustered together, the subject hub lead will mentor the new subject leader in their role. Teachers are then targeted for a school-wide development project using the ARC model. This may be to lead an initiative across the school, such as the introduction of retrieval practice. The school-wide assignment helps develop a broadening understanding of pedagogy and practice beyond the teacher's own key stage expertise. The school-wide assignment also develops opportunities for the teacher to build relationships with a wider group of colleagues.

As the teacher progresses, opportunities to become a research champion or research coach emerge and they move from research coachee to research coach. At this stage in our talent pathway programme, the teacher is heading towards becoming an expert teacher. Expert teachers are encouraged to share their practice, including research practice, across the school and beyond. Formal training routes are offered to the expert teacher, including the Chartered College of Teaching Chartered Teacher or Leadership course and the National Professional Qualification for Middle Leadership or Senior Leadership.

The development of the expert teacher within the advanced teacher talent pathway allows teachers who are keen to remain class-based to share their expert knowledge of pedagogy, practice and research with others. I have also found that clearly articulating the opportunities outlined in the advanced teacher talent Pathway motivates teachers to aspire to develop their research practice and take greater ownership of their own career pathway.

LEADERSHIP PATHWAY

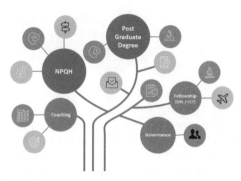

Our expert teachers who are interested in developing their leadership skills are supported through our leadership pathway. Future leaders are offered a 360° leadership review where a range of staff are asked to review the teacher's leadership qualities. This review gives the fledgling leader a perspective on their leadership through the lens of other staff. The data from this is analysed by the leader and a coaching conversation is then held with a senior member of staff. Opportunities for training are developed, including sponsorship on the National Professional Qualification for Headship (NPQH). Wider opportunities are given for teachers to work across schools within the trust and beyond through our network of schools. We have a national support school in our trust, bringing opportunities for leaders to share their expertise across a wide network of schools, thereby building strength in system leadership. Leaders are encouraged to share their research outcomes with other organisations through training events, such as conferences and TeachMeets. Our leaders are encouraged to share their research findings and practice through presentations such as 'LeadMeets' and publications online such as blogs and articles.

Teachers on the leadership pathway are given opportunities to become a lead research coach, using group coaching to support the development of teachers in their team (Britton, 2010). Wider leadership skills are provided to future leaders through school and trust-wide assignments using the ARC model. Assignments may include running a research training programme for staff across schools or developing an element of research practice within a team of teachers. In the past two years, 12 teachers have been supported on the leadership pathway and, as a result, three teachers have been promoted to leadership positions within trust schools. There is, however, a note of caution here. In developing some teachers through the leadership pathway, other teachers not targeted for development can become demoralised and may perceive themselves as left behind as they see their colleagues promoted.

GOVERNANCE PATHWAY

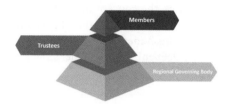

Highly effective governance is key to the quality of education in our schools. Our governance pathway ensures our governors are supported in developing the necessary skills for their role. Governance is developed through a wide range of training opportunities. The skill set of governance is key when building a culture and climate of research. In my trust, we have appointed several trustees and governors who have a strong record in research practice. This ensures that the vision for research across our schools is fully supported by governance. The Research Cycle can be used with governors to guide their own inquiry into outcomes for pupils. Governors who understand the Research Cycle can also monitor the impact of research across the organisation, building a layer of quality assurance into the Research Cycle.

RESEARCH PATHWAY

Building a culture and climate within the school where research is valued and applied by all staff takes tenacity. In order to maintain a keen focus on research, we introduced the research pathway. As a research-active organisation, we provide time for our teachers to engage in a research project each year as part of their appraisal cycle. Each teacher is coached by their team leader to devise a purposeful research question. Teachers are given a 'learning ticket' with a value of £150 to support their research activity. Teachers can spend this on relevant courses and professional membership of organisations such as the Chartered College of Teaching to support the teacher's research activity. If the research project requires further financial support, teachers can apply for a research bursary with a value of up to £500 to assist their research project. One of my teachers on the research pathway used their research bursary to purchase a set of Lego to research the impact of using Lego to support narrative development in boys' writing. I will explore the concept of the learning ticket and research bursary in more detail later. We have found that through our research pathway, each research project brings fresh ideas and opportunities for teachers to share their practice with others, deepening the teacher's own professional standing in the school.

Teachers are guided by their coaches to engage in TeachMeets and journal clubs to develop their engagement with pedagogy and practice. Teachers with similar research questions are grouped together in professional learning communities to work collaboratively on their research project (Tan and Hairon, 2016). The research pathway supports teachers in developing their research methodology. Through this, a research-informed culture is built across schools where teachers bring fresh ideas to their practice and test these out through reflective inquiry.

The talent pathways system motivates staff to develop practice and take greater ownership of their own career pathway. This has been demonstrated through the analysis of staff questionnaires and feedback given by teachers undertaking professional development within our talent pathways and during group coaching sessions.

Talent pathways have created a culture of professional development in my schools, creating a climate where teachers feel valued and are empowered to take increasing ownership of their own professional development. A wider benefit of talent pathways is the retention of teachers, with a reduction of teacher resignations across our trust in the past two years from 19% in 2018 to 6% in 2019 for our 32 teachers. While the introduction of talent pathways cannot be credited as the only contributory factor to the retention of teaching staff, teachers state in staff surveys that they feel more supported in their professional development as a result of our talent pathways. Talent pathways therefore strengthen succession planning, growing future leaders within our schools and making schools within our trust increasingly future-proof and failsafe.

If you are considering developing talent pathways as a system to develop professional development and strengthen research practice, here are my seven key steps:

- Create talent pathways **personalised to your school** by reviewing your current professional development and research opportunities for each staff group in your school.
- Consider the **training gaps** and whether any other organisations can support you.
- Train your **senior staff to coach** teachers through the talent pathway (Chisnell and Jordan-Daus, 2020).
- **Assign coaches** to spot talent in teachers, encouraging teachers to take on assignments and research projects, build relationships and attend relevant courses.
- Support the teacher through their talent pathway with **regular coaching sessions**.
- **Learn from what works** and review your pathways.
- **Celebrate success** across the organisation.

Coaching

Coaching, in its myriad of guises, offers the researcher the scaffolding needed to raise a superstructure of practice. The coach will help guide the researcher to understand themselves, deepen their awareness of roles and responsibilities, build clarity of thinking and become a deeply reflective practitioner. Embedding a culture of coaching in your school is key to empowering your researcher to gain the most from their research practice. I will now explore some of the most helpful elements of coaching that help to embed a culture of research.

APPRECIATIVE INQUIRY

Our appraisal system starts with the concept of appreciative inquiry (Cooperrider et al., 2011) at step 1 of the Research Cycle. This is a powerful concept as you act as research coach, supporting your researcher to define the issue upon which their research question will rest. Too often in schools and organisations, we focus on what is not working well. While this mode of working helps firefight problems, it is a deficit model. The firefighting approach can misdirect your researcher to try to fix something rather than innovate using their personal strengths. The appreciative inquiry model flips the deficit model on its head and starts from a point of strength.

Appreciative inquiry differs from problem-solving techniques used in organisations as rather than focusing on an analysis of causes to a problem, the process asks the participant to enter a dialogue to envision what might be.

The first step of appreciative inquiry is to ask your researcher a positively powerful question (Whitney et al., 2010). This question could be, 'Tell me about one thing you have undertaken this year that you are particularly proud of.' This question asks your researcher to think about their personal pride and strength. It also connects them to the organisation. Too often, staff in schools are asked to account for what has not been achieved. Appreciative inquiry turns that culture around and starts with what has been achieved. Whitney et al. suggest five traits of appreciative inquiry that resonate with embedding a culture of research in schools:

Inquiry – ask positively powerful questions that encourage a dialogue about an individual's strength. With research in mind, asking positively powerful questions opens up your researcher's thinking. Possibilities are widened as there is an optimistic element to this discussion.

Illumination – highlight the best in people and in situations in order to learn from what works. This can then be used to apply to other situations that require further work. It is our natural default to be reluctant to sing our own praises, but this process permissively dispels this and actively encourages the researcher to be appreciative of their own strengths and the strengths of others.

Inclusion – engage with groups within your organisation to help co-author the future. In the context of research, I apply this to grouping together researchers who have a common theme to their research questions. This helps to build collaboration and relationships across staff groups.

Inspiration – awaken the creative spirit of staff. In research, this is created in the Research Cycle as the possibilities created by an inspiring research question emerge.

Integrity – make choices for the good of the whole. In the Research Cycle, the positive impact from sharing research findings across the school and beyond builds integrity in the organisation as staff build a confident belief in how their research work benefits students, staff and the wider organisation.

Using appreciative inquiry as a coaching tool provides a platform upon which a meaningful research question can form at step 1 and step 2 of the Research Cycle. The research coach needs to be trained in the skills of appreciative inquiry, and the process and purpose needs to be explained to the researcher. Direction and permission need to be given in order to stop negative or deficit statements creeping into the conversation. The research coach needs to be astute and draw their researcher back into positive statements, should the need arise. There is plenty of time to focus on the barriers or pitfalls at a later stage in the Research Cycle. In the formative stages of the discussion about the researcher's issue and emerging research question, thinking about the barriers or difficulties in practice too readily can stop a train of thought that leads to the ideal research question.

Appreciative inquiry encourages talk about success. It builds relationships with the researcher and their coach and across the wider organisation through embedding a culture of positively powerful questions. It raises participation of staff who are motivated by these conversations. It also helps build a positive vision of the future of the organisation through the formulation of meaningful research questions.

Here is an example of how appreciative inquiry supported a teacher researcher in my school. Jane was thinking about how to inspire a reluctant group of children to engage in maths. She was a year 1 teacher and had just inherited a new class with a small group of children who were struggling with basic number facts. Rather than think about what the children could not do, I asked Jane the question, 'Tell me what subjects you love to teach.' Jane's face lit up as she spoke to me about her love of stories and how she used stories in writing lessons to inspire the children and how stories were used in history to bring the lessons to life for the children. I then asked Jane if she could think about using her strengths and passion for stories in the context of maths for this group of reluctant children. Jane paused. I love this moment with researchers as the pause often indicates a moment of deep thought or revelation. Jane looked at me after a few moments of deep reflection and said, 'In my many years as a teacher, I have never thought about using stories in a maths lesson.' This set Jane on a journey towards a research question about how stories can influence mathematical understanding. So, from a simple appreciative inquiry starting point, the researcher is led by their own strength and interest to a purposeful research question that has the potential to impact on their own practice and the practice of others.

MENTOR-COACHING

I first came across mentor-coaching as a tool for developing staff in 2006. I was trained along with a group of headteachers by Roger Pask and Barrie Joy from the London Centre for Leadership in Learning to deliver mentor-coach training across the county. The mentor-coaching system (Joy and Pask, 2007) is an holistic process to empower the mentee-coachee to think through unresolved issues in their professional life and to navigate a path through them to a positive resolution.

The principles of mentor-coaching can also be applied across a range of strategies in school and can have a profound impact on the development of school staff. I have used the principles of mentor-coaching in delivering the Research Cycle. The basic premise of the mentor-coach cycle is outlined here:

Mentor-Coaching Cycle

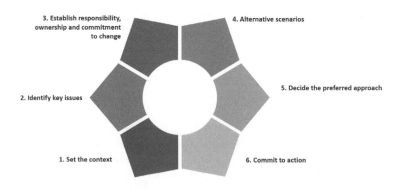

In training staff to use these principles, the culture of the school develops and empowers a climate of openness and trust amongst staff. The skills in mentor-coaching can be applied to the role of the research coach as they develop their capacity to help the researcher to think through their research at each step of the Research Cycle.

The first stage of the mentor-coach cycle asks the mentor to listen. The key in guiding your researcher to their research question also begins here at step 1 of the Research Cycle. Mentor-coaching techniques centre on asking great or Socratic questions, echoing the principle of appreciative inquiry's powerful question. As mentor to your researcher, you need to ask questions that help you understand your researcher's context. You need to leave your assumptions at the door and build your skills of empathy to get as close as possible to understanding what it is like to wear your researcher's shoes. In doing this, it is also important that you recognise that you will never be able to fully empathise with your researcher; however, effective questioning will help you get close to understanding their thoughts, feelings and beliefs that relate to their context.

A powerful tool I use when coaching is silence. In accepting that there will be periods of silence in your conversation with your researcher, you provide space to think – both for you to think of powerful questions and for your researcher to think about their own response. Too often, we feel compelled to fill the silence with chatter. This can often misdirect a conversation or close down thinking. When we experience silence, we often feel compelled to speak after around three seconds. As a research coach, you need to rehearse the skill of remaining silent before this becomes habitual. I have found that explaining that there will be silence in the conversation – and that this is often where the deepest thinking takes place – dissipates the awkwardness of any eventual silences.

Listening is also an essential skill for the research coach. A good research coach will listen without trying to bring their own solutions to the researcher. The feeling of being truly listened to builds a powerful and positive relationship between research coach and researcher. In order to become a great listener, you need to fully attend to your researcher. You must, as far as possible, cast out distractions and limit interrupting your researcher's train of thought with your own interjections. Turn off your phone, shut the door, and explain that this time is sacrosanct. This can be a challenge for staff in school, but affording the time for research coaching gives an important message that the organisation values the research process. By attending to the conversation, you allow your researcher to lose themselves in their thinking and find new possibilities. Be cautious to also make sure that your researcher owns the conversation. Listen attentively to what is being said and just ask questions at this stage to allow your researcher to find their own pathway to their research question.

It is far too easy for the coach to hear a researcher grappling with an element of their practice and to jump in with a solution to the perceived issue. The coach can easily jump in with a solution or a comment such as 'Oh that happened to me! I know exactly how you feel about that!' In these situations, the researcher will often close down the conversation as there is little point in progressing their ideas of research as the answer is already 'known' by their coach. Be cautious not to proffer solutions or sympathise with your researcher.

The final skill I encourage our research coaches to develop is to listen without note taking. The act of writing notes while your researcher is talking can be distracting. Rather, I encourage our appraisers to listen intently, ask questions and punctuate the conversation with review checks. A review check may take the form, 'So what you have told me so far is that you are really proud of your practice in maths but you are now grappling with how to apply what you have learnt to your new cohort of children. You are not yet certain of the direction of research but think it may be around strategies to help your more able children to flourish. Have I got that right?' This helps summarise as you go and helps your researcher crystallise their thinking.

Earlier in the book, I considered cognitive bias in the research process. It is worth reminding ourselves at this stage that in building a culture of research, as a research coach, you must maintain an awareness of how cognitive bias impacts on your researcher. The research coach needs to use questions to test out potential cognitive bias in their researcher. Powerful questions are needed that challenge slow or lazy thinking. A researcher may state, 'There is no point focusing on that group of children because they will never catch up.' The astute coach may then ask a question to challenge this bias by asking, 'Is there anything in your own unconscious bias that causes you to think this?' This simple question asks the researcher to question their initial statement and challenge their own unconscious bias. Questioning has the great potential to challenge lazy thinking and help your researcher develop as a reflective practitioner.

GROUP COACHING

Group coaching in its many formats has been a tool used by business and education sectors for some time. Britton (2010) defines group coaching as 'a small-group process throughout which there is the application of coaching principles for the purpose of personal or professional development, the achievement of goals, or greater self-awareness, along thematic or non-thematic lines'.

While there are many models to group coaching both in industry and in education, I find Sir John Whitmore's 'GROW' model helpful (Whitmore, 2017). The GROW model for group coaching is explained as follows:

- **Goals** – what do you want to achieve?
- **Reality** – what is happening now?
- **Options** – what are your options ahead?
- **Way forward** (or **What will you do**) – how are you going about it?

Building a culture of group coaching within school provides a helpful platform for staff within teams or research groups to work collaboratively to develop research practice. Group coaching helps staff to improve outcomes for students or colleagues through shared reflection and dialogue (Clutterbuck et. al, 2016).

Using the group coaching model, a lead research coach is assigned to each group coaching session. The coach is a non-hierarchical role that changes with each session. The research coach leads the questioning and timing of the discussion based on the GROW model. The session begins with the coach encouraging the researchers to bring an unresolved issue in their professional life to the discussion. This is then unpacked with the view of creating a potential research question for the member of the team. The coaching session then develops to the 'reality' phase, where the questioning teases out the reality of the context faced by the member of staff. This helps the researcher define their context and why this issue is relevant to their potential research.

The research coach then draws the researcher to think about their options, asking key questions to elicit thinking about how their research question is likely to impact on future practice. Finally, the research coach helps the researcher to construct the way forward as they envision the future impact of their research on their own practice.

At each stage in group coaching, the coach facilitates the discussion, offering questions themselves and encouraging questions to be asked by colleagues. As the group coaching session develops, the coach then gives permission for the other members of the group to offer possible solutions and ideas to the researcher, which they can either take on board or dismiss. As with all effective coaching sessions, the researcher is left feeling empowered, as they own the direction of their discussion and are supported to reflect on their own ideas without being told what to do by others.

The group coaching model can be used at any or every step in the Research Cycle to support research practice. By building a culture of coaching for staff, the school becomes an organisation where staff become increasingly confident in their research practice. As a result, the climate or feel of the school is enhanced as research practice becomes an integral part of school life.

When developing the role of the research coach in your school – whether using appreciative inquiry, mentor-coaching or the GROW model – training is vital. The research coach needs to be well versed in the Research Cycle in order to best support their researcher and competent in the theory and practice of coaching in order to bring value and integrity to the coaching role. Developing coaching skills takes time and builds with experience. Once mastered, the role of research coach brings a powerful dimension to the development of a culture of research in schools.

Learning tickets

As we touched on earlier, learning tickets are a way for researchers to take ownership of their own professional development. We asked our staff, 'What would you do if we transferred £150 to your bank account to spend on your own professional development and research?' This began the concept of the learning ticket. Each learning ticket is worth £150 and our staff are given this to spend on their research practice. Some staff use the learning ticket to join professional organisations, such as the research-focused Chartered College of Teaching, while others sign up to subject organisations such as The Association for Science Education. Staff have used the learning ticket to buy train tickets to visit schools outside their area, and others used it to fund books and journals relevant to their research. When I introduced this concept to my trust business manager, she came back to me with an ashen face as she calculated the collective cost of providing this for all our teachers from our professional development budget. Nonetheless, we introduced the system and found that by the end of the year, the amount spent on professional development fell. That's right: fell. We discovered that by giving the ownership for professional development to our staff, they spent the budget far more purposefully. The attendance at one-off courses fell, and the benefit of a year-long research project led to lasting improvements in our system. This was truly a win-win scenario.

At the point of appraisal, our researchers are encouraged to spend their learning ticket wisely. And while we don't give them a cash transfer into their bank account, they can draw on this ticket across the year, provided this links to their research question. The learning ticket gives a powerful message to our staff that their research is valued and the school supports their research work, enhancing the climate of research across the organisation.

Research bursaries

Research bursaries were likewise mentioned earlier in the book, and we will now explore them in more detail. While we provide learning tickets to support the research of our staff, there are times where this is not sufficient. For this reason, we offer research bursaries. A single member of staff can bid for up to £250, but two or more working collectively on a research project can bid for up to £500. This encourages joint submissions and collaborative research projects to emerge across the schools. As an example, a member of staff wanted to trial the use of Lego in developing narrative in reluctant writers in year 1. The research bursary allowed the teacher to purchase the Lego kit in order to undertake the research project. The research impacted positively on the target group of reluctant writers and the research outcomes were shared across the school, establishing the use of Lego as an intervention for developing writing in reluctant writers.

Another example of the use of the research bursary was seen in a teacher who used the money to purchase tickets to travel between states in the USA during a summer trip. This allowed the teacher to meet up with teachers and district superintendents to research the different approaches to teaching early phonics. With a bit of creative thinking, the teachers in these examples brought research outcomes that were initially out of reach to the school through the support of the Research Bursary. Like the learning ticket, the research bursary opens the mind of your researcher to engage in a research project that was initially unfeasible, helping them to take their research to a deeper level.

Time

Engaging and embedding a culture of research in school takes time. The Research Cycle helps the researcher manage their time as it provides a year to engage in their research activity. It is also important for school leaders to recognise and value the time research takes in staff and to consider the additional workload research can create. If you are to build a culture and climate for research in school, careful thought must be afforded to creating time for this to take place.

In English schools, teachers are entitled to five training days each year. As research-active schools, we hold three face-to-face training days and then give two days back to our researchers. This equates to ten hours of self-directed research time that we ask our teaching staff to engage in throughout the year. This payback of time gives an important message to our staff that their research work and workload are valued equally. I do not doubt, however, that many of our teachers spend far and above the designated ten hours on their research practice. Giving time reduces the heat of the work, allowing staff to choose when and how intensively they work on their research practice. In managing this time, the researcher can work at their own pace, and the research itself also benefits from it.

In order to demonstrate the commitment to research for our non-teaching staff, we pay for an additional day's employment. This gives our non-teaching staff an extra five hours for their research work. Like our teaching staff, this time gives a powerful message to our staff that we value them and their time spent on research. As an organisation, it also demonstrates that there is an expectation that all staff engage in research practice as this is a paid element of their professional development.

Research groups – training teams

Helping staff understand the methodology of research is key to embedding a culture of research in schools. Using the Research Cycle, we target groups of staff to engage in a year-long programme of research training. The training follows the Research Cycle and introduces staff at every level to the process of research. The group meets six times through the year to support their understanding of the theory behind the Research Cycle and practice it develops. The training helps staff build a solid foundation to their research practice and fosters strong relationships between staff as they develop their practice together.

I run a research group for our early-career teachers.. Teachers can be drawn from within one school or across schools. Groups can focus on those teachers with similar research questions or diverse questions. In bringing early-career teachers together, teachers begin to develop their research practice, they learn to question one another and build a shared understanding of the Research Cycle that builds a confidence in research practice that will endure for the remainder of their career.

I run a research group for teaching assistants who are aspiring to become research coaches in our schools. The group of teaching assistants was formed using the trust's talent pathway programme to target staff who demonstrated a passion and aptitude for research. Once these members of staff have been through the training programme, they are assigned as future research coaches for colleagues, building talent and capacity for research for years to come. Building capacity across the organisation to replicate the training programme is an important step to building a culture of research in school. This ensures that the culture of research doesn't rest on one person, but rather if one key person leaves the organisation, the culture of research is sustained.

Research training can also take place across leadership teams. This can involve both curriculum and business teams in larger schools and trusts. Leadership research training allows the research methodology to focus on generic leadership issues that span all leadership groups across the organisation. Leadership research training brings a diverse dimension to the research discussions and broadens all our leaders' perspectives on the varied roles and responsibilities across our schools and trust.

Research groups provide opportunities to train staff in the methodologies within the Research Cycle that help embed a strong culture of research across the organisation. This creates the climate of confidence in research practice where staff feel increasingly secure in sharing their research outcomes with others both within and beyond the organisation. Be creative in how you introduce research groups, as drawing together the right group of staff to become future research coaches and research champions can empower their research and help build the culture and climate of research in the organisation.

Professional learning communities

I first came across professional learning communities on a trip to Singapore. The professional learning community is a group of teachers who have been brought together to use research to inform practice and collectively improve outcomes for students. I sat in on a professional learning community discussion in a Singaporean secondary school. The discussion was led by an expert teacher and the science teachers present were given a data set from recent tests for their students. The expert teacher then drew upon a journal article and led a discussion relating the article to what the data suggested was happening with their student learning. This led to the teachers brainstorming ideas of how they could adapt their practice in light of the article and discussion points. The teachers were then charged with trialling a range of ideas and returning to the professional learning community with the outcomes of their action-research.

The professional learning community model has been adapted into many formats globally. For me, the key to this model is to draw like-minded staff together either within your organisation or from beyond in order to focus on a key research question. The collective mind on this research question can give multiple perspectives to the research activity, providing the researchers with different context to their studies as they test out a new practice within the context of their own roles and responsibilities.

The structure of the professional learning community brings about opportunities for staff to gather together with a collective research aim. This is an engaging and purposeful model for research-informed practice within schools, bringing together the use of talent pathways where school leaders target staff for professional development by providing opportunities to be lead coach in a professional learning community.

Another practical use of the professional learning community is to group together a team at the point of appraisal. With a group appraisal discussion, a team of staff can be coached to work together to define the issue relevant to their team that can be nurtured into a meaningful research question. The professional learning community is then formed to follow one research question. Staff within the professional learning community then work through the Research Cycle together. This is a powerful system for teams in the school that may struggle to find a range of research questions. As an example, in one of my schools, the cleaners worked within a professional learning community to research systems to engage pupils in taking greater ownership of taking pride in the cleanliness of their toilets. The team worked together on the shared research question 'Does making children aware of toilet hygiene reduce workload for cleaning staff?' The cleaning team learnt about child psychology, environmental issues relating to hygiene and products to improve the toilet environment as they explored step 3 – 'Review what is known' – of the Research Cycle together. Through the professional learning community, the staff were able to support one another to navigate the Research Cycle and share the pride in their research findings. The team were also able to lean on one another when sharing their findings, building confidence in research and strengthening relationships.

As a final word of caution, it is worth reminding ourselves of the dangers of lethal mutation (Wiliam, 2018) discussed earlier in this book. The intent of professional learning communities goes far wider than a research brief alone; however, the concept remains a valuable one to apply to research practice in schools. As such, be aware that when I refer to professional learning communities in the context of research, it is a victim of lethal mutation and one I believe to be a positive evolution from the original concept.

Research buddies

The research buddy system is a simplified version of the professional learning community. In my schools, I group the research undertaken by curriculum staff into broad themes. Within these themes, I produce a bubble map that groups the names of colleagues who are undertaking similar areas of research. I then share the research buddy bubble map across the trust, encouraging staff to make contact with others undertaking similar areas of research. These are research buddies. Here is an example of a research buddy map for a group of teaching assistants across my trust. The research buddy map links researchers undertaking similar (within the bubble) and linked (overlapping bubbles) research activities. Research buddies are encouraged to share their research questions and support one another in step 3 of the Research Cycle by sharing their findings of what is known about their research issue. Research buddies can also work together to co-design their research methodology as step 5 of the Research Cycle. I have found that research buddies sometimes adapt their research question together to focus on different yet complementary dimensions of research. An example of this is where two teaching assistants, looking into the effect of speech and language provision on four-year-olds, elected to study different genders to enable them to compare their findings and draw wider conclusions from their aligned research questions.

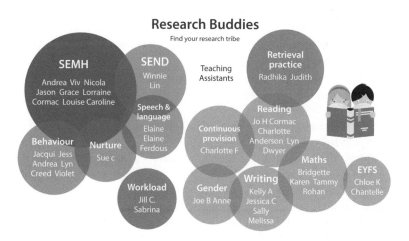

Research buddies provide a structure in which staff are empowered to self-regulate their support for research. In sharing the Research Cycle with colleagues, researchers in school draw from one another's ideas and enthusiasm and gain from the experience. It has also helped staff to build confidence in step 7 of the Research Cycle as they work together with their research buddy to co-present their research findings to the wider organisation.

Research champion

In order to build a culture of research in school, the research champion plays a pivotal role in developing a commitment to research within all staff groups. The research champion is a role that supports the culture of research in school by nominating a staff member to be a 'champion in the ranks'. In creating research champion posts within the school, whether it be a designated position or a role within a wider job description for an existing member of staff, you send out an important message to the wider staff body: 'We value research at this school.'

The research champion needs to have a strong passion for research, knowledge of research methodology and the Research Cycle, and they need to be an effective coach that is confident to speak in public. It is worth appointing a Research Champion for the key teams across the school. In doing so, the capacity for research is built and the research champion group can support one another in the development of research practice across their teams.

Here are the key roles and responsibilities for our research champions:

- Actively engage in research practice through the Research Cycle and be seen as a **champion of research** in your team.
- **Regularly review progress** towards research-based appraisal targets for staff in your team, providing support for research methodology to strengthen outcomes.
- **Provide links to research** for staff and build opportunities for staff through the trust's research pathway.
- **Support the publication of research outcomes** for staff, including the production of blogs, research papers and research journals.
- **Coordinate events** across and beyond the trust including TeachMeets, journal clubs and research training events.
- **Publish research** and best practice on the trust website.
- **Support and train staff** in understanding research methodology.
- Develop opportunities for staff to engage in **professional learning communities** and with **research buddies** to enhance their research practice.

The research champion provides the school with a member of the team that embeds research practice in the culture and climate of the school. They work as coach to other team leaders and staff to keep the conversations about research alive and relevant. The research champion also strengthens that inextricable link between the organisational values and research, maintaining the purpose and momentum of research in your school. Choose your research champions wisely as they have the potential to support you in embedding a culture of research in your organisation.

Speed reading – Buzan

I have used Tony Buzan's system of mind mapping as a teacher, university lecturer, headteacher and coach (Buzan, 2009). It wasn't until relatively recently in my meandering life that I came to the revelation that my reading speed was not limited to the pace of the voice in my head.. I knew my wife could read a book in a fraction of the time that I could with my steady reading pace. We began speaking about the different approaches to reading that we both took. While I subvocalised and sounded out words in my head, she rarely did this. While I read dutifully from left to right, she would scan a page left to right, right to left and sometimes even from top to bottom of a page, allowing the words to flow into her eyes while her brain deciphered the meaning. This, for me, was a revelation. While I had the skills to skim a document for relevant meaning, I was often seeking key words or phrases rather than taking in relevant information. I then discovered Buzan's approach to speed reading.

In The Speed Reading Book (Buzan, 2010), Buzan explains the system of learning to speed read, a skill that is so often simply acquired rather than taught in our schools. I am happy to say that I now have the capacity to read with great efficiency, taking in articles, books and journals with increased speed and with greater retention of key information.

Buzan outlines a range of techniques that help your reading accelerate. The first step to speed reading is to understand that in order to read faster, you need to still the voice in your head. This is called subvocalisation. When we subvocalise, we sound out the words we read in our head, thus slowing us down to a rate of speaking. When reading, we need to learn to still this voice in order to speed up.

The second step in speed reading is to take in increasingly large chunks of words. When we read, we tend to read in groups of words, taking chunks of three or more words in one glance and allowing our brain to connect these words. Training yourself to chunk more words helps you speed up. Once these skills of subvocalisation and chunking are mastered, the reader is ready to power up their reading by applying a range of different scanning techniques. Buzan suggests nine different scanning techniques to help speed reading. These include reading two lines at once, scanning left to right then returning right to left. While this all sounds curious, with practice the system really works.

I keep a copy of The Speed Reading Book on my bookshelf and lend it to researchers who state they find reading laborious. Speed reading is a great skill to gift to your researchers as they embark on stage 3 of the Research

Cycle – reviewing what is known. While reading fast in itself does not make a more astute reader, it does help the researcher to navigate through lengthy and sometimes complex texts to glean the key elements of meaning. This allows them to develop their skills of reading for relevance at step 3 of the Research Cycle and later in step 6 of the Research Cycle as they practise the skills of eyeballing their written data.

TeachMeets

My first experience of a TeachMeet was in London. I visited Quintin Kynaston Community Academy to speak about introducing a poetry slam in school. I was given a strict time slot of seven minutes where I had to deliver my message. It was a thrill and a challenge. The limited time given to the presentation really sharpened my mind as I had to think about how to get the key points of my presentation across. The format followed that of a TED talk and even had the digital countdown to keep me to time. The range of presentations given were inspiring, delivered by teachers who spoke about their practice and pedagogy. I was hooked.

I introduced TeachMeets across a local network of schools. Teachers met together in schools and at times in a local pub, where we encouraged staff to share and discuss their practice. This format was inspiring for staff who attended, so I then worked with a colleague from Canterbury Christ Church University to replicate this across a wider network of schools. It was at this point I realised that the TeachMeet was a great platform to share research outcomes. I held our first trust research TeachMeet at The Pines Calyx, a beautiful venue in St Margaret's at Cliffe in Kent. Staff were encouraged to present their research findings and we welcomed 26 presentations to the stage that day. The pride felt for my staff was palpable, as presentations shared the research stories from a diverse range of staff. Presentations varied from the business manager presenting on the impact of appreciative inquiry on her team to a teaching assistant presenting on precision teaching and a teacher presenting on mindfulness research. Each presentation provided an insight into the research undertaken across the schools. As staff listened and formed questions, they were able to share in the research practice of their colleagues, while growing their own practice as a result of the research-informed presentations. My hearty recommendation is to find a TeachMeet, LeadMeet, BrewEd or researchED event and go.

As a school leader, setting up a TeachMeet within your school is an important step to becoming outward facing with your research practice. Gathering a group of researchers within your school who are willing to share their findings is the first step. The TeachMeet can also be held as a departmental meeting, staff meeting or whole-school training session. The rules are simple. Decide on the allotted time for each presentation. Ask for any slides to be forwarded to you prior to the TeachMeet. Have a lead to introduce the presentations and another to keep participants to time. I use a set of increasingly large school bells that I ring if the presenter goes over time. This adds a little humour to the process and allows the presenter to wrap things up without feeling they are being tugged from the podium by a metaphorical shepherd's crook. I also like to hold a raffle to add some fun, with prizes being a couple of academic books and some stationery.

In planning a TeachMeet, McGill (2021) provides a helpful guide on his website. Here are some of his key points when planning for a TeachMeet:

Date and timing – think about the venue, school calendar, and who is available to help organise and present. Ensure you build in plenty of time to gather and confirm speakers. Also consider the time needed to advertise the event and book in delegates.

Venue and facilities – consider whether to use your own school or to hire another venue. Using your own school is simple as you will be aware of the logistics this involves but using another venue can provide a more neutral space if inviting delegates from beyond your organisation.

Social media/hashtags – social media can be a powerful tool. It can be used to promote the event and encourage engagement by delegates and speakers. Bear in mind that social media is open to the public and as such can be seen by all. Remind those involved in the event to remain professional at all times. You can also use a hashtag to link to your event but be cautious: hashtags, like everything on social media, can be misused.

Websites – if your school has a website, this can be used to advertise your event and be the front window for any documents, blogs or resources linked to the TeachMeet. This is also good for encouraging staff from beyond your organisation to see your commitment to research-engaged work.

Prizes and donations – ask around in your workplace or on social media for donations for prizes. The wider your TeachMeet, the greater chance your event will attract organisations willing to offer prizes. Teacher-authors are also a useful link as they may be willing to offer a free book, particularly if they are presenting at the TeachMeet. During the event, plan for how you will give out the prizes. This could be a raffle or an award for the best tweet or comment made about the event.

Hosts – it is important to find a host, or hosts, that can carry the event. I find that having two hosts is helpful as this builds professional banter and the hosts can keep one another and the speakers on track.

Presenters – think carefully about who can present. You may have a theme to your TeachMeet and this can guide who you approach to present. The TeachMeet is usually a volunteer-led event. As such, presenters will not expect payment. However, if your presenter is travelling and requires overnight accommodation, you may need to consider a budget to cover this. You may also want to have a keynote presenter to draw a wider crowd of delegates.

Resources and reminders – build a clear to-do list. This keeps you on track and ensures all bases are covered. You may want to produce a programme of events for delegates to follow.

Arrival and directions – keep this simple, offer clear directions to the venue and have guides ready to direct delegates once at the venue. Think about parking and transport issues and remember to reserve parking for those helping with the event.

Check-in – the front-of-house greeting is really important. This settles delegates and presents a professional feel to your TeachMeet. Have a team of helpers as guides and offer ID badges on arrival. This makes delegates feel welcome. The event booking can be undertaken using a digital event booking tool that will create delegate badges on arrival, giving that welcome feel.

Thank-yous – during the event, remember to thank those who have made this possible, from presenters to caretakers. Follow up the event with formal thank-yous. You may even like to offer a thank-you gift to presenters as they leave the stage.

TeachMeets – or their other manifestations, such as researchED and BrewEd events – offer a great opportunity for your researcher to share their research findings. These are grass roots organisations jam-packed with keen educationalists brimming with fresh ideas about pedagogy and practice.

Building on the TeachMeet, I hope to see an increasing prevalence of TeachMeet-style events forming for our non-curricular staff in schools as a springboard to showcasing the research practice of the wider school staff.

Journal clubs

Journal clubs provide a forum where staff meet to review a journal article. This can be an activity in its own right or be part of a professional learning community. The research champion selects a journal article that is relevant to the group and shares this with the participants. The research champion will then read the article prior to the journal club, highlight key phrases and pose key questions to share at the journal club. Staff then meet – usually with coffee and cakes – and are given a copy of the journal article. The participants are given time to read the article, although some may have chosen to read the article prior to the session. (I provide highlighters and pens at this stage.)

The research champion then leads a discussion on the article, posing questions like:

• What **resonated** with you when reading this article?
• Is there anything within the article that particularly **surprised** you?
• Do you **agree** with the author's perspective on this practice?
• Was there anything in the methodology chosen for this study that is **flawed?**
• Can you spot any **cognitive bias** in this article?

I find that journal club discussions swiftly take on their own life as participants begin posing their own questions and making their own observations, relating the article to their own experiences and educational context. I run journal clubs within my schools but often offer these out to colleagues beyond our trust, bringing a wider perspective of educational context to our discussions. Through modelling questioning, the research champion acts as research coach and supports the researchers to be critical when reading a journal article, developing an analytical eye to aid their review of what is known in a given field of study at step 3 of the Research Cycle.

Journal club is a powerful tool to use with a group of researchers who have similar research questions as this can help them review what is known relating to their emerging research question. It builds relationships across staff teams as they come together to engage in professional discussion about practice. Journal club also offers an opportunity to mix staffing groups as the journal article may relate to an organisational issue that is relevant for both curriculum and business leaders within the school. Equally, a journal article discussing student wellbeing can be relevant for teaching staff, lunchtime supervisors and pastoral teams. The research champion or research coach needs to think carefully about the choice of article, how accessible it is for the participants and its relevance in order to ensure the researchers gain the most from the journal club. Journal club can also include an article written by a current staff member. As I have mentioned, we produce a journal for our trust that publishes the research undertaken by staff. In sharing their article with colleagues, the researcher is able to support the school to adapt and affirm practice as a result of their research findings, bringing deep value to the sharing of research findings across the organisation.

Reading groups

The reading group is similar to a journal club. However, while a journal club focuses on an article, the reading group focuses on a broader text or idea. The reading group brings together a group of researchers interested in a similar theme and, like the professional learning community, encourages that group to meet regularly during a full Research Cycle. The reading group will often focus on a book as this gives a wider opportunity to unpack the ideas being presented, discuss them in the group and then try out the ideas for themselves. The reading group can provide a group of researchers with the chance to discuss the writing of an author in depth and engage in research trials from the ideas discussed in the group.

The reading group is best structured using a research coach. The coach groups researchers with similar interests, using the research buddy bubble map to guide the groupings. The research coach then brings a relevant text to the group and encourages the group to read a specific chapter in the book in order to promote discussion. The reading group meeting can take place face to face or as a virtual meeting. The research coach brings a range of pre-prepared questions relating to the chapter or text to stimulate discussion. Questions could include:

- What are the **key ideas** in the chapter/book?
- Which ideas **resonate** with you or your research question?
- Are there any issues or ideas that **challenged your thinking**?
- How could you **apply** the approach described to your setting?
- What **changes** to your practice would be needed in order to apply the principles in this chapter, if any?
- Can you think of any **potential barriers**?

- Can you spot any **cognitive bias in the text?**
- Can you spot any **cognitive bias in yourself** reading this text?
- How has this text **changed your thinking**, if at all?
- Do you have **any questions** that remain after reading this article?
- Are there any issues in this text that are relevant to **your research question?**

Reading groups, like professional learning communities, can boost the relationships between staff and build a culture of research across the school. The regular timing of the reading group meetings can also help maintain the pace of research across the school for those involved and build a constant conversation about research that permeates through the organisation.

Conclusion of chapter 3 – 'Creating a culture of research'

Building a culture of research in schools involves setting up and delivering a range of systems and programmes that build an infrastructure in which research takes place for all staff. Systems such as introducing the Research Cycle, embedding research practice into the school appraisal system, training staff in the research methodology, and linking staff through professional learning communities and journal clubs all support the culture of research in school. While the process of building a culture of research in school is complex, it is even more challenging to maintain this and ensure research practice is embedded across the organisation.

If the culture of research is to become embedded, the systems must rest on the shoulders of many across the organisation. Building a system of research where there are multiple research coaches who can champion research across the teams within a school is key. This multifaceted approach to research creates a critical mass in developing a lasting culture of research in school. Systems like talent pathways in research practice help to grow future research leads and build an infrastructure of research which is resilient to changes in staffing.

By embedding a culture of research in school, the climate of the school becomes one, where staff are inquisitive and interested in their own practice and the practice of others. Staff feel listened to and valued. Their professionalism swells as their research practice develops. Relationships strengthen through opportunities for collaborative work relating to research practice. If the culture of research is embedded in a school, the climate follows, and the school becomes an organisation where staff are keen to belong.

Key messages from chapter 3
'Creating a culture of research'

- The research **culture** of the school involves the structures and systems put in place that support research practice.
- The research **climate** of the school involves the relationships between staff, how safe staff feel, the physical environment, their joy of teaching, love of their role, feeling valued and a feeling of love for the school; climate is the heart and soul of the school.
- In creating a positive culture and climate of research in schools, school leaders need to develop a culture of **followship** where staff connect with the purpose and vision for research.
- Appraisal provides a helpful framework for embedding a culture of research in schools. The **appraisal cycle** gives the researcher a clear timeframe and framework upon which their research can take place.
- Building talent pathways for staff, especially a **research pathway**, provides a powerful roadmap for embedding a culture of research in school.
- Effective **research coaching** helps to embed a culture of research in schools. Coaching skills need to be developed in staff using models of coaching such as **appreciative inquiry**, **mentor coaching** and **group coaching**.
- **Learning tickets** and **research bursaries** support research practice across the school, providing a clear statement of financial commitment to research practice for staff.
- If research is to be embedded in the culture and climate of a school, **time** must be given to enable staff to engage in the Research Cycle.
- **Research groups** support the formal training in the Research Cycle, ensuring staff fully understand each step of the process.
- **Professional learning communities** offer a helpful focus in drawing together staff undertaking similar research practice, building organisational relationships and discussion about research practice.
- **Research buddies** offer a useful tool to link staff undertaking similar fields of research in the school.
- It is important to develop reading skills in researchers, including the strengthening of reading for meaning and **speed reading**. This helps staff to review what is known about their research issue and to develop the skill of eyeballing their research data.
- **TeachMeets** – or their other manifestations, such as researchED or BrewEd events – offer a great chance for researchers to share their

research findings and connect with like-minded colleagues both within and beyond their organisation.

- **Journal clubs** and **reading groups** create a helpful forum to embed a culture of inquiry in school. They build relationships across staff groups and allow research coaches to model research practice.

Conclusion

In writing this book and devising the Research Cycle, I have learnt some key points about building a culture of research in school. Firstly, that if you get the culture (what you do) for research right in your school, the climate (how it feels) will follow. The Research Cycle empowers staff to become researchers as the process of research is demystified, leading to all staff engaging in research practice, building a self-improving organisation where staff are empowered to lead change.

Research in schools, however, has its difficulties and limitations. Finding time to undertake research is a deep challenge, as is staff confidence. Overcoming these two hurdles is a worthy quest for the school leader as they can both become a block to embedding a culture of research. Be courageous, keep the end goal in sight and remember to celebrate the wins along the way while learning from the bumps in the road. As an 80-year-old interviewee on Radio 4 said when asked for advice for the prime minister who was about to celebrate his 50th birthday, 'Entering your fifties is a little like getting into the sea while on holiday. The thought of it is a little chilling, but once you're in, it's lovely.' I encourage you to dip your toes into the sea of research – and I assure you, once you are in, it is indeed lovely!

Irresistible Learning website

If you would like to find out more about how to engage in research practice, visit my website, Irresistible Learning. The site offers a range of resources that will support your research journey.

www.irresistiblelearning.com

Bibliography

Alexander, R. (2020). A dialogic teaching companion. Routledge.

Buzan, T. (2009). The Mind Map Book. BBC.

Buzan, T. (2010). The Speed Reading Book. BBC.

Blakesley, S. J. (2012). Performance at the highest Level. GMC Publishing.

Britton, J. (2010). Effective Group Coaching. Friesens.

Cambridge Primary Review Trust. (2020, May 6). CPRT Research. Retrieved from CPRT: https://cprtrust.org.uk/research

Cambridge. (2013). Cambridge Advanced Learner's Dictionary Fourth Edition. Cambridge.

Chartered College of Teaching. (2020a, May 6). Research Engagement Toolkits. Retrieved from Chartered College of Teaching: www.my.chartered.college/resources/research-engagement-toolkits Accessed: March 2021.

Chartered College of Teaching. (2020b). *Chartered College of Teaching home page.* Retrieved from Chartered College of Teaching: www.chartered.college Accessed: March 2021.

Chisnell, G. (2021). Talent Pathways – building a culture of career development in schools. Impact 11:33-36.

Chisnell, G. and Jordan-Daus, K. (2020). We're all in this together. Using a peer coaching model to support middle leaders' development. Impact 9:50-52.

Clark, A. (2005). *Beyond Listening: Children's perspectives on early childhood services.* The Policy Press.

Clutterbuck, D., Megginson, D. and Bajer, A. (2016). Building and sustaining a coaching culture. Chartered Institute of Personnel Development.

Cooperrider, D. and Srivastva, S. (1987). Appreciative inquiry in organizational life. In Woodman, R. W. and Pasmore, W. A., *Research in Organizational Change And Development. Vol. 1.* Stamford, CT. JAI Press, pp. 129-169.

Cooperrider, D. L., Sorenson, P. and Whitney, D. (2001). *Appreciative Inquiry: An Emerging Direction for Organization Development.* Stipes Publishing LLC.

Dabell, J. (2020). *Research Myth 7: Brain Gym.* Retrieved from Teacher Toolkit: www.bit.ly/3vypkQZ Accessed: March 2021

Didau, D. (2015). *What if everything you knew about teaching was wrong?* Crown House Publishing.

Dimmock, C. (2019). Leading Research-Informed Practice in Schools. In D. A. Godfrey, *An Ecosystem for Research-Engaged Schools.* Routledge pp. 56-72.

Education Endowment Foundation. (2020). *EEF Home.* Retrieved from EEF: www.educationendowmentfoundation.org.uk Accessed March 2021

Education Endowment Foundation. (2020, May 6). *The Education Endowment Foundation.* Retrieved from EEF: www.educationendowmentfoundation.org.uk Accessed March 2021

Hairon, S. and Dimmock, C. (2012). Singapore schools and professional learning communities: teacher professional development and school leadership in an Asian hierarchical system. *Educational Review Vol 64*, 405-424.

Hyerle, D. (2011). *Student successes with thinking maps.* Corwin.

Joy, B. and Pask, R. (2007). *Mentoring-coaching a guide for education professionals.* Open University Press.

Kahneman, D. (2011). *Thinking, fast and slow.* Penguin.

King, R. (2016). *Singapore's Education System Myth and Reality.* Insight Press.

Lovell, O. (2020). Sweller's *Cognitive Load Theory in Action.* John Catt Educational.

McAleavy, T. (2016). *Teaching as a research-engaged profession: problems and possibilities.* Education Development Trust.

McGill, R. M. (2015). *Teacher Toolkit: Helping you survive your first five years.* Bloomsbury.

McGill, R. M. (2021) Planning a TeachMeet: start to finish – TeacherToolkit. www.bit.ly/3aRcchY Accessed: March 2021.

Nicholas, L. and West-Burnham, J. (2018) Understanding Leadership – challenges and reflections. Crown House Publishing.

NYU Libraries. (2020, July). *NYU Libraries.* Retrieved from How to create a research poster: www.bit.ly/3eGuG5N Accessed: March 2021.

Oxford. (2020). Retrieved from oxfordlearnersdictionaries.com. Accessed: March 2021.

Pease, A. and Pease, B. (2017). *The definitive book of body language.* Orion.

Robinson, K. (2009). *The Element.* Allen Lane.

Robinson, M. (2013). *Trivium 21c: Preparing young people for the future with lessons from the past.* Independent Thinking Press.

Royal Society. (2019). *Harnessing Educational Research.* The British Academy.

Ryan, W. (2008). *Leadership with a moral purpose.* Independent Thinking Press.

Sweller, J. (1998). Cognitive load during problem solving: Effects on learning. Cognitive Science 12:257-285.

Tan, S. and Hairon, C. (2016). Professional Learning Communities in Singapore and Shanghai: implications for teacher collaboration. A Journal of Comparative and International Education 1-14.

Thomas, G. (2017). *How to do your research project – a guide for students.* Sage.

West-Burnham, J. (2009). *Rethinking educational leadership.* Continuum.

Whitmore, J. (2017). *Coaching for Performance.* Nicholas Brealey.

Whitney, D., Trosten-Bloom, A. and Rader, K. (2010). *Appreciative Leadership.* McGraw-Hill.

William, D. (2018). *Embedded formative assessment.* Solution Tree Press.

Zeni, J. (2006). A guide to ethical issues and action research. *Educational Action Research 6:1*, 9-19.